UNLIMITED GRACE

The Power of Christ Within

∼

James A. Kirkwood

Copyright © 2006 by James A. Kirkwood

Unlimited Grace
by James A. Kirkwood

Printed in the United States of America

ISBN 1-60034-528-X

All rights reserved solely by the author. The author guarantees all contents are original and do not infringe upon the legal rights of any other person or work. No part of this book may be reproduced in any form without the permission of the author. The views expressed in this book are not necessarily those of the publisher.

All Scripture references are the author's translation from his lifetime of Bible studies.

Cover photo courtesy of National Aeronautics and Space Administration (NASA).

www.xulonpress.com

DEDICATION

To my wife, Mary Lachen Kirkwood, whose love for God and His Word has inspired me, whose love for me God has used to help Him keep my head above water during the flood times of life. She encourages me to trust God and to attempt the unthinkable with His help. Without that encouragement, I would not have written this book.

ACKNOWLEDGMENTS

Thanks to my editor, Bethel Kirkwood Franklin, who doubles as my daughter. Her hard work, understanding of grace, and excitement over this project have helped immeasurably.

And a special thank you to the following for their expertise and helpfulness: John and Wendy Kirkwood, Bob and Denise Cat, Karen Peterman, Paul Siebold and numerous other friends whose labors, patience, prayers, and many kindnesses have helped to make it happen.

PREFACE

This book was written for you. It has a life changing message for the saved and the lost, the young and the old, the new believer and the veteran. It also has vital truths for the child and for the scholar, the seeker and the skeptic, the hopeful and the hopeless.

Every author has a special reason for writing a particular book. My reason is simply to help the reader to find answers to the confusing issues that trouble every single life — issues that plagued my own thinking and hampered my own living for years. This book is meant to read like a conversation between you and me. God loves you, and if I knew you, I would too. You might even love me — with some special help from the power of Christ within you. Don't believe a word I say in this book until you check it out in Scripture. God is the sole authority in all matters of our faith and walk. I hope that I have said nothing in this book that would give you unnecessary offense. Let's be friends! I'm human, too. If necessary, cut me the slack that friend cuts for friend. Our little conversation is about many things thought controversial, but *Christ* is controversial, thank God! And His Grace is, too.

I send this book forth with the prayer that the reader will find blessing on every page. If it blesses you, share the blessing with others.

Meet you in the clouds!

Duke

CONTENTS

1. A New Beginning 13
2. Two Births 21
3. Two Lives 29
4. Keys to Bible Understanding 37
5. Sin in the Life of the Believer 45
6. Feeding the New Dog 53
7. Why Us? 61
8. Standing and State 67
9. Getting It Straight 75
10. Two Programs 83
11. Two Gospels 91
12. Two Invitations 99
13. Two Ways 107
14. Two Goals 115
15. A Thousand Oaks 119
16. Learning to Live 125
17. Why Church? 131
18. Seated with Christ 139
19. God Works in You 147
20. New Power for a New Life 153
21. Unlocking Time 159
22. Power in Prayer 169
23. The Mystery 177
24. Rightly Dividing the Word of Truth 187

CHAPTER ONE

A NEW BEGINNING

~

So, you are now a Christian! I wasn't there when you became one, but I know just how it happened. God's Word told you that "...God commendeth His love toward us, in that while we were yet sinners, Christ died for us."[1] You believed it and were saved. Many other things may have taken place. You may have put your total trust in Christ's complete saviorhood alone, on your knees, in your bedroom, or on your feet in a crowded football stadium. An evangelist may have told the crowd that "Christ died for our sins,"[2] or you may have heard it from a relative, a neighbor, or a friend. You may have wept when "it" took place, or laughed aloud with a new happiness. But, make no mistake, it is when you trusted Christ's death for YOU, for YOUR sins, that the miracle of your new birth took place. When the Philippian jailor asked Paul, "What must I do to be saved?", he answered, "Believe on the Lord Jesus Christ and you will be saved."[3] Powerless sinners do all the believing;[4] Almighty God does ALL the saving...it's as simple as that. "The gospel is the power of God to salvation to EVERYONE who believes."[5] Always, in Scripture, salvation comes by Grace alone, through faith alone, in Christ alone![6]

God tells us clearly that salvation is His work and His alone. Our part is to do the only thing we can do without "doing" anything...to trust in what another has done. All of us need, first of all, to realize that OUR fingerprints are nowhere to be found on our salvation.

It is completely and eternally a work of God for us, and NEVER our work for Him, in whole or in part. God wants us to know this because if salvation were our doing, Satan would soon "undo" it. Because it is wholly a work of God for us, IT CAN NEVER BE UNDONE![7]

One of the keys to understanding our new life is to RECOGNIZE the difference between salvation and service. In the Bible, discipleship is always costly, salvation is always free.[8] The Greek philosopher and the Hebrew rabbi alike charged their students tuition. So did Christ. He said that no person could be His disciple, follower, or student unless he put Him ahead of father, mother, wife, husband, son or daughter. Yes, said Christ, even ahead of one's own life. Way ahead! To offer your entire life to the Lord is the highest tuition you could possibly pay, but you can only do this *after* He has saved you instantly, completely and eternally, by His grace.[9]

When man tells us that we must do something to be saved or stay saved and uses a discipleship verse to prove it, he is confusing salvation with service. God always distinguishes them, and so must we. Salvation can and should produce worship and service. Worship and service CANNOT and DO NOT produce salvation! Religion always gets this wrong. The Bible always gets it right!

You've never heard of a fireman rescuing someone from a burning building and then throwing that person back in because he didn't say "Thank you," failed to buy tickets to the Fireman's Ball, or threw a brick through the Firehouse window. A rescue is a rescue. Christ didn't die to be your probation officer, but to be your Savior.[10] Not to give you a second chance, but a new and eternal life. Not to throw the door of Heaven open so that you might struggle through, but to seat you permanently in Heaven with Him.[11] It's all by Grace or it's not by Grace at all.[12]

Now that you're saved, you have an entirely new and different life. It won't be problem-free and it will certainly present new and greater challenges than your old life did. But, God has made a perfect provision for every believer's life and ministry. The ancient Israelis took forty years to make a journey that required only eleven days. They brought a lifetime of unnecessary suffering and grief upon themselves. This book is designed to help YOU to avoid years of wandering in a barren desert of constant and repeated defeats and to help you find God's purposed way of victory and peace.

Life is full of complicated problems to which the Bible has simple, though not always easy, solutions. Determine to be like God – solution-conscious. Begin immediately to make *your* life a life of Bible study. Our Lord told our arch-enemy that "Man shall...live by every word that proceeds from the mouth of God."[13] Success Motivation Institute defines success as "the progressive realization of a worthwhile pre-determined goal." Make your number one priority the daily intake of Bible doctrine. Don't pick your church the way most others pick theirs. Sit under the very best teaching you can find and persist in your lifetime commitment to personal Bible study. Salvation is instantaneous. In a split second you believed God and passed out of death into life.[14] Christian life is progressive. You will never outgrow your need for sound Bible teaching. We can never have too much doctrine, though we can employ too little.

And remember, God's Word, properly grasped, ALWAYS produces greater and greater love — love for God and love for others.[15] God and Peter say "Unto you therefore who believe He is precious."[16] Believe what? Believe the information God gives to us in HIS Word about the person and work of our Savior. If we have only a little information (sound Bible doctrine), we will view Christ as somewhat precious. If we have more, He will be more precious. If we have a lot, He will be most precious. Remember, we were made *by* Him and *for* Him. We exist for Him, not He for us. Our happiness cannot be greater than when it is totally subordinated to His happiness. "It is God who works in you to will and to do of His good pleasure."[17]

So, your new beginning gave you a new and different life. Life is to be lived and we must *learn* to live it. A newborn baby learns by experience. A cry brings food, a dry diaper, or attention. Then he learns by observation – he sees parents and siblings meet challenges in certain ways. Then he learns by instruction – do this, don't do that. And finally, he learns by reasoning. As in the physical, so it is in the spiritual. We are "born again" and begin almost immediately to learn in a variety of ways. Hopefully, we will learn from divine revelation the most important things, "spiritual things communicated by spiritual means."[18] The most important things can only be taught us by God Himself in His own unique and inimitable way – through the Bible rightly divided. Teaching is God's job; learning is ours.[19] The Word of God is like a diamond mine; some of its gems lie just inside the entrance in plain sight. But some of its greatest treasures lie deeply hidden and only yield themselves to hard labor – diligent study.

The first secret for you, as a believer, to learn is that God's Word is more necessary to your spiritual life than physical food is to your body. "Man shall live...by every word that proceeds from the mouth of God." You are a citizen of Heaven on loan to Planet Earth[20] and the success of your mission will depend on the health of your soul. Your number one priority is the regular, daily intake of sound Bible doctrine. As with your physical food, ingest it, metabolize it, and utilize it daily, hourly, moment by moment. Scripture must become the rhythm of your new heart, the breath in your spiritual nostrils. There are many Christians who have died wishing that they *had* lived *for* Christ; none that having done so regretted it. The believer's life as God designed it is not to be lived for self, but "unto Him who died for us and rose again."[21] A lifetime offered in sacrifice to a loving God is never wasted.[22] C.T.Studd, the world-famous athlete and missionary, said, "If Jesus Christ be God and died for me, then no sacrifice can be too great for me to make for Him."

Howard Ferrin, for many years the president of Providence Bible Institute/Barrington College, used this illustration. There was a captain of a 19th century sailing ship whose son begged him repeatedly to take him to sea. One summer day, the captain did, making his young son his cabin boy. Now the son begged his dad to let him climb the main mast which towered seventy feet above the deck thrusting its very top into the broad Atlantic sky. "All right son," reluctantly agreed the father, "but you must promise one thing: all the way up and all the way back down you must keep your eyes on the top of the mast. Never look around; the tilting of the horizon will make you dizzy and faint. Most of all," said his father, "resist the temptation to look down at the ship. The sight will frighten you, rob you of your strength and could even cost you your life."

The young cabin boy, new to rolling, pitching ships and tossing, rushing waves began his climb. Not familiar with the rigging, a stranger to the great struggle of the climb, aware of the seeming endlessness of the mighty ocean, he nevertheless enjoyed the exhilarating boldness of the sea breeze, the call of the gulls, the scent of the air.

A feeling of confidence swept over him, born of his sense of achievement as the awe-inspiring mast surrendered to his little frame with its giant will. "It won't hurt to take a look around," he thought as he passed the crow's nest and neared the pinnacle of his adventure. The sky was bluer than he had ever seen it and the clouds as white as snow. Off in the distance was the horizon rising and falling like a great see-saw.

"What a sight! If only the horizon would lie flat and still." But it wouldn't. He sensed a growing weakness in arms and legs where, just seconds before, his own strength had surprised him. His breath came more quickly. Hands that had gripped ropes confidently now clung desperately. Wanting security, he looked down. It was the wrong place to look. Below, the now tiny ship swung out from under him, first to starboard then to port. The crew appeared like ants along the ship's rail, his usually huge father incredibly small against the distant deck. How could the safe haven of such a large ship have become so frighteningly small?! Terrified, the boy grasped the ropes, his hands and feet numbed by his fear.

Far below him the captain, seeing his little son's plight, cupped his hands and shouted with all his might, "Look up, Son! Look up!" and again, "Look up, Son! Look up!"

Taking a deep breath, the boy obeyed. Suddenly there it was – the top of the mast. It had been his helper on the way up and now it brought him comfort in his time of greatest need. The nausea left him. Breathing became normal and strength returned to once quivering arms and legs. The top was reached, a moment to rest and descent began. The long climb down went steadily, not quickly. The flush of victory brought back color to his cheeks, rhythm to his breathing, a pleasant excitement to his heart.

If we look around us at the constantly shifting horizon of other believers in their wavering see-saw of victories and defeats, we will grow dizzy and distressed. If we look down within ourselves at all our weaknesses, failures, and sins, we will be frightened and faint. We must always look up to Him who never fails us, never changes. The climb will belong to us and the victory will be sweet.

Christ is the top of our mast. Nothing will enable us to maintain our occupation with Him like studying, believing, understanding, and applying His Word.

CHAPTER ONE NOTES

1. Romans 5:8
2. I Corinthians 15:3
3. Acts 16: 30-31
4. Romans 5:6
5. Romans 1:16
6. Ephesians 2:8-9
7. Romans 8:31-39
8. Romans 6:23
9. Luke 14:26
10. Hebrews 7:25
11. Ephesians 2:4-6
12. Romans 11:6
13. Matthew 4:4
14. John 5:24
15. II Thessalonians 1:3
16. I Peter 2:7
17. Philippians 2:13
18. I Corinthians 2:13, lit.
19. John 6:45
20. Philippians 3:20
21. II Corinthians 5:14-15
22. Romans 12:1-2

CHAPTER TWO

TWO BIRTHS

∼

Something happened! Something happened and you are not the same. You did the only thing that a person can do without "doing" anything – you trusted Christ and you were born again.[1] It will help you to understand your second birth if you know something about your first.

Once upon a time a haploid from your daddy's body met and married a gamete in your mom's body and you were conceived. The sperm cell with 23 chromosomes, united with the ovum, also having 23 chromosomes, and formed you. You began life as a somatic cell, a cell with 46 chromosomes, 23 from Daddy and 23 from Mom; but you weren't just any somatic cell, you were a zygote, a cell unlike any other cell in the Universe. The cell contained a "blueprint" that would decide whether you would be male or female, blue-eyed or brown, brown-haired or blond. Everything that goes to make up the present you was in that cell just awaiting development. If you were just a part of your mother's body you would not have half of your chromosomes from Dad. You would not have your own DNA, you would have Mom's, and Mom's blood type, which you may or may not have. You never have been part of your mother's body, but you were a guest in her womb. And since she chose to keep you alive and to nourish and protect you, here you are – a uniquely wonderful creation of God, and Dad, and Mom.

Your spiritual birth bears some similarities to your physical birth — and many differences. One similarity is that in your first birth two forces united to produce one unique you. The Spirit of God and the Word of God also united to create one unique you, this time "born from above" (lit.), "born of God."[2]

All human beings ask the same questions: Who am I? Where did I come from? Why am I here? Where am I going? Some Americans upon completing college took these unanswered questions to the Far-East hoping for answers, but came home with none. Acres of diamonds! The answers were right there in the Book their grandmothers read!

Where did you come from? From Mom and Dad immediately, but mediately from Adam. And Adam could only produce "after [his] kind," or genus.[3] Fallen Adam could only produce fallen progeny. So you and I started life with a fallen Adamic nature. That's the bad news. The good news is that when you were born of God you received a new nature, a divine nature. Sinless! And incapable of ever becoming other than sinless! So, here you are — one person with two natures, two bents, two inclinations, two capacities, two sets of likes and dislikes. If you thought your troubles were over when you trusted Christ (I thought so!), think again! Our troubles were just beginning.

Of course, we should never forget for even one minute that we were hell-bound and hell-deserving. We were headed for Gehenna, the garbage dump of eternity. Now you and I, well, we're headed for an eternity of unimaginable and unlimited bliss in a very real place that God's Word calls Heaven. We were on the road to Hell when the grace of God intercepted us and "the God of all grace" gave us eternal life as a totally free gift, bought and fully paid for by His Son upon His cross. Never lose sight of where God brought you from and where He has brought you to. This is a great key to consistency in your life and ministry. Remembering what a gracious God has freely given you and the awesome price His Son paid for you to have it will keep you stable in a world that is coming apart at the seams.

So, we have a few problems. So what! God has a solution to every one of the believer's problems, and His solutions are clearly stated in His Word. Actually, we Christians have only *one* problem. Lewis Sperry Chafer identifies our one problem as "adjustment to the indwelling Spirit."

> "Two natures dwell within my breast;
> One is cursed, the other blessed.
> One I love and one I hate;
> The one I feed will dominate."

Harry Ironside, in his youth a missionary to the Indians of the great Southwest, was riding with a dear friend, an Indian chief. The chief said, "Harry, I have two dogs in my bosom and they're always fighting." "Which one wins?" inquired Ironside. "The one I feed," said the chief.

So, how do we help the good dog win? We feed it the Word of God! "Man shall....live by every word that proceeds from the mouth of God."[4] This was Christ's prescription for spiritual success and He has shared it with us. Of course as we feed the new nature, the old will starve. It won't die this side of Heaven, but it will be weaker than the new. It will still give us a battle, but it will be less powerful than "the dog we feed," and life will be increasingly characterized by our honoring God rather than disgracing Him.

Now, we desperately need to know that when our new birth gave us a new nature something else happened — something we need to understand to live life as God designed it to be lived by all believers. And that "something" that we must know is this: the person that we were before we trusted Christ has died legally as far as Heaven's court is concerned. The person we were "in Adam" no longer exists.[5] Our old nature still exists as long as we are in this body, but the person we were when we were united to fallen Adam has no legal standing with God. In other words, I am no longer old Jimmy, condemned. I am now new Jimmy, justified. No one can be condemned by God and justified by God at the same time.[6] I have the problem of being a saved person in an unsaved body (with its unsaved nature), but I do not have the problem of standing condemned before God, nor can I ever again have it! No one – man or angel – can successfully place a charge against the believer. God tells us emphatically that

He Himself cannot charge us with a sin for which Christ died. And Christ died for all of the believer's sins.

> "My sin, oh the bliss of this glorious thought,
> My sin, not in part but the whole
> Is nailed to the cross and I bear it no more.
> Praise the Lord. Praise the Lord, oh my soul."[7]
> – H. G. Spafford

My sin, not in part but the whole was nailed to the cross. Not in part, but the whole! "He by Himself purged our sins."[8] Christ, on His cross, paid your entire debt, and God never collects a debt twice! "He paid a debt He didn't owe, because we owed a debt we couldn't pay."

Once, as I began to tell a hitch-hiker the good news that Christ died for our sins, he snapped, "Christ died to throw the door of Heaven open." This is what his church had taught him from his childhood, but it is not the teaching of Scripture. The Bible knows nothing of a Savior who only dies to make salvation possible. The Bible's Savior "is able to save them to the uttermost that come unto God by Him, seeing He ever lives to make intercession for them."[9] Everywhere in Scripture Christ dies to save the sinner instantly, completely, and eternally. To the uttermost!

The Word of God knows nothing of a "savior" who doesn't save, but only gives us a second chance, a clean page to write on, a fresh start. Whether salvation is viewed through justification, redemption, reconciliation, propitiation, regeneration or any of the other benefits of Calvary, Christ always saves completely and never part way or for a time! "He that believes is not condemned."[10]

The believer, as God views him, is not someone who must work, run, or fight his own way into Heaven because someone has only thrown the door open. In the Bible, every member of the Body of Christ has been seated with Christ in Heaven. You and I walk the Earth, but "our citizenship is in Heaven." We are not striving to enter a door open only wide enough to admit struggling pilgrims saving themselves with the help of religion or a church. If you and I believe, God saves. That is the promise of God.

All Christians believe that Christ died for sinners; few Christians believe that they died with Christ. Union with Christ is the most important teaching of Scripture for the believer to study and embrace. It is sadly the least known teaching in the Word. The Bible says that Christ died for sinners. The same Bible says, with equal emphasis, that we believers died *with* Him.[11] The first truth is necessary to our salvation, yours and mine. The second is essential to our living and ministering for Christ. The all important union of Christ and the believer begins at Calvary. It does not begin in a tank of water, but on a cross. When we trust Christ, the Holy Spirit "incorporates" us into Christ forming a union that cannot and will not ever be broken. "I am [lit. "was and remain"] crucified with Christ,"[12] says Paul, and makes plain in chapters 6 and 7 of Romans that this co-crucifixion is not limited to the Apostle himself, but is also true of us, of you and me. "Christ died." The church readily accepts it. "We died with Him." At this, the church frequently stumbles and sometimes falls.

How could you and I be said to have died with Christ when His death took place centuries before we were born? Because the death He died was *our* death; He had no death of His own to die. Death had no claim on Him. But God only applies the benefit of that death to us at the moment we believe.

The Savior not only died *for* our sins but *to* our sin – to our sin nature.[13] Again, He had no sin, and no sin nature. He died to our sin nature. He died for the things we do, but also for the persons we were. And we died with Him to the person we were without Christ. John Wesley said, "Never think of yourself apart from Christ." Good advice. No, *great* advice! My "old man" was Jimmy without Christ. My "new man," the person I have been since my new birth, is Jimmy *with* Christ! And it will always be so! This is why God never again views us as in Adam, where He could only see us as condemned, but always sees us as in Christ where there is no condemnation.

> "Near, so very near to God;
> Nearer I could not be.
> For in the Person of His Son,
> I am *as near as He*."

On your worst day as a Christian, in the precise moment when you committed the worst sin you, the believer, ever committed – perhaps one "you wouldn't want Mother to know,"— God was occupied with viewing you as you are in Christ, and not as you were in Adam. Knowing that is not an incitement to sin, but an inducement to holiness!

Paul gives us his motive for living "all out" for Christ when he says, "For the love of Christ constrains (impels) us, because we thus conclude: that if One died for all, then all died; and He died for all, that those who live should no longer live for themselves, but for Him who died for them and rose again."[14]

Calvary in Scripture is never merely to produce a race of people incapable of ever going to Hell and certain of Heaven — it does that — but to produce a race of people who cheerfully and eagerly abandon their selfishness in order to live for Christ! Grace, when actually grasped, *always* produces worship and service. Grace is the greatest motivation to true holiness that this Universe will ever witness. It is God's grace that enabled Him to slay the person you were in sin and under condemnation, and "birth" a new you, faultless before His throne.

CHAPTER TWO NOTES

1. John 1:12-13
2. John 3:3
3. Genesis 5:3
4. Matthew 4:4
5. Romans 6:6
6. Romans 8:33-34
7. From the hymn "It is Well With My Soul" by H. G. Spafford
8. Hebrews 1:3
9. Hebrews 7:25
10. John 3:18
11. Romans 5:8; 6:8
12. Galatians 2:20
13. I Corinthians 15:3; Romans 6:10
14. II Corinthians 5:14-15

CHAPTER THREE

TWO LIVES

"If you take people out from under the Law, they'll sin!" The Pastor had his "business face" on and was using his "business voice" as he leaned forward, eyes narrowed, and sold his point with a look. He said this in spite of Romans 6:14, where God plainly says, "You are not under Law." God says we are not under Law; the Pastor says we are. "Houston, we have a problem!" "Law," without the definite article in Greek refers to law in general – that which has the quality of law. But law in general includes "*the* Law" of which the Pastor spoke. God didn't stop with saying, "You are not under Law," but He continued, "you *are* under Grace." If Law were superior to Grace, God wouldn't put believers under Grace now, would He? But Law is *not* superior to Grace; Grace is superior to Law. Infinitely superior!

Romans chapter six makes it clear that the Law never broke the back of sin; Grace did! The Law is a set of externals operating on man from without, and given to man in the flesh. "Those that are in the flesh *cannot* please God."[1] The Law never removed one sin nor saved one sinner. The Law is a package; it doesn't just say, "You shall not commit adultery,"[2] it says, "the adulterer shall surely be put to death."[3] It doesn't just say, "You shall not murder."[4] It says, "Kill murderers!"[5]

Grace is the power of Christ within!

> "Do this and live, the Law commands,
> But gives me neither feet nor hands.
> A better word the gospel brings;
> It bids me fly, and gives me wings."

The Law of Moses/Law of the Lord is perfect, but it can neither save nor sanctify; it was not designed to do either. It was designed to reveal to man that he has a sinful nature.[6] Before the Law was given man was quite conscious of his sins, (plural), but not of sin (singular). The Law forbids things that the flesh loves to do, and enjoins things that the flesh hates to do, exposing the reality of indwelling sin.[7] When the Law had done its work in the publican, he cried out "... Be propitious to me, *the* sinner."(lit.)[8] Law reveals the corruption of our inner beings and proves to us that the Law cannot change our natures.[9] Therein lies the Law's perfection. Far from being a defense attorney, it is a perfect prosecutor, a perfect jury, a perfect judge, and a perfect executioner. If you attempt to stand before a righteous God in the "filthy rags"[10] of your "doing," the Law will roll over you like a steamroller and crush you like a grape!

We are a race of rebels. What makes a rebel a rebel? His rebellious nature. It is the nature of a rebel to rebel. Try putting a sign on your front lawn in front of your picture window and pile some baseball size rocks around the sign. Paint the sign to read, "DO NOT THROW ROCKS THROUGH WINDOW!" A word of caution: don't sit in the living room. Retire to a safe spot and wait for the crash of a rock and the tinkle of broken glass. Wasn't the sign a good sign, legible and easily understood? Yes! Didn't you have a perfect right to place the sign there? Of course you did! But prohibitions arouse rebellion in the heart of a rebel. People who have passed your house 1,000 times and never felt the urge to be destructive may find the urge suddenly overwhelming and irresistible. There was nothing wrong with your law against rock throwing. Nor is there anything wrong with God's commandments. Paul calls them holy, and just, and good, and spiritual, and glorious! But a good law is bad news to bad people. A holy law is bad news to unholy people. A just law is bad news to unjust people. A spiritual law is bad news to carnal (fleshly) people....well, you get the idea.

Loretta lay dying in Gottlieb Hospital. Skin and bones, with a face that resembled a skull, not the pretty face that she once had. She did not attempt to hide her obvious terror at the thought of her impending death, now only hours away. "Loretta," I said, "I used to think that Heaven is a reward for good people, but studying the Bible has convinced me that Heaven is a gift for bad people." "Pastor," she responded, "you must be kidding!" Her shock was apparent. We turned to Romans 6:23 where we read together, "The wages of sin is death, but the [free] gift of God is eternal life in Christ Jesus, our Lord." "Loretta, what are wages?" I asked. "Something we've earned," she replied, "something we have coming." "Right, Loretta, now what is a free gift?" Her wide eyes grew suddenly wider, she struggled to sit up in bed, using the last of the strength in her emaciated body. "I see it!" she fairly shouted, "I see it!" In that instant she was born again, born from above, born of God. Her eternal destiny forever changed from the wages we all deserve to the gift freely given – bought and paid for by Christ.

The Law shows lost sinners that we are lost sinners and that the only hope for lost sinners is the pure, uncompromised grace of God.

Since no one can be under two such diametrically opposed systems as Law and Grace, we must die to the one to live in the other. Romans chapter seven is the classic declaration of this great fact. The woman of verses 1-3 would be properly identified as an adulteress if she took a second husband while the first was living. But if the first husband dies, she is completely free from the law that bound her to him. She is now dead to that law and free to marry another man. She was slain to the marriage law by the death of her husband. Verse 4 tells the Romans that the death of Christ brought an end to their old relationship, freeing them to be united to Christ risen and glorified in order that they might bear fruit to God. Grace is *always* liberty to serve, never license to sin!

"The Law was not made for a righteous person,"[11] and so could not have any claim on Christ. Christ came voluntarily under the Law.[12] He was conceived under Law, born under Law, raised under Law. He lived under Law and died under Law. But when He died, He died to the Law and all who died with Him died to the Law also.

When He rose, He rose above and beyond Law and so did we who rose with Him.[13] It is as simple as that!

The person you were before you trusted Christ alone for your salvation no longer exists. That person was totally and properly lost, justly condemned, hell-bound and hell-deserving. That person was clothed in the filthy rags of human righteousness and had only a fallen, sinful, Adamic nature. That person was abiding under the wrath of God. All these things and many more were true of you before salvation, but they *are not true of you now*. The person that went into the tomb with Christ is not the same person who came out of the tomb with Him!

Galatians 2:20 is much loved and frequently quoted by God's people, but unfortunately often misunderstood. Let's look at it. It reads, "I am crucified with Christ: nevertheless I live; yet not I, but Christ lives in me: and the life I now live in the flesh I live by the faith of (in) the Son of God, who loved me, and gave Himself for me." In our English versions the verse begins with "I," (the 'perpendicular pronoun')... "*I* am crucified." But God never wrote a word in English, and in the Greek in which God and Paul wrote Galatians, the verse begins with "Christ" and not with "I." What's the difference? Simply this. The first century Greek writer did not have a computer with which to print in **bold** for emphasis, and he didn't use underline, or *italics*. He would put the most important word or phrase first in the statement to give it primary emphasis. The last word or phrase would have secondary emphasis, and in between these two emphatics many interesting things could happen. The most emphatic word in Galatians 2:20 is *"Christ"*! "*Christ* I have been crucified with." When was Christ crucified? About one third of the way through the first century A.D. This proves that co-crucifixion with Christ is not "an experience to be sought by all Christians" and enjoyed by some. Nor is it an experience to be had by all of us in the future. In Greek, the perfect tense always refers to an action completed in time past with present day results. To do it justice in English we would have to say, "Christ I was completely crucified *with* in time past and remain so today." Our co-crucifixion with Christ is not something that could happen, may happen, should happen, or shall happen; it is something that DID HAPPEN then and is still in force NOW, and can never be diminished or undone.

Next Paul tells us, "yet I live." Permanently crucified, dead, but still living! How can this be? At Calvary Christ ended the first stage of His human existence – His life in humiliation, and began the final and eternal stage – His life in glory. Christ was buried for three days and then rose out from among the dead, beginning His resurrection life, and Paul's, and yours, and mine! True, Paul's *physical* resurrection is still future as is ours, but we rose spiritually out of death and into life when Christ rose, and we share His resurrection life already. Now. Right now! Scripture says, "For in that He died, He died to sin once for all; but in that He lives, He lives to God. So *also you*, acknowledge yourselves to be *actually dead to sin*, but *alive to God* in Christ Jesus our Lord."[14]

Now, and only now, God and Paul add the exhortation, "Stop allowing sin to reign as king in your mortal body, for you to obey it in its desires."[15] Verse 13 comes after verses 11 and 12 because the knowledge that we *must have* to enjoy victory over sin in our *experience* is the knowledge that God has *already* broken the reign of sin in our *position*! We *cannot* end the reign of sin through our human life – the flesh life – but we can through our resurrection life – our life in Christ.

You and I, trusting in Christ crucified, buried, and risen for us, were only united to Christ as "the Man of Galilee," "the Lowly Nazarene," briefly – on the cross. Since His resurrection, our union with Him has been a union with Him risen and glorified. We are not branches in a vine, but we *are* members in a body. Think of it!

Having told us that he had been slain with Christ, but that he lives still, Paul adds, "no longer I." The Paul who died on the cross with Christ is not the Paul who still lives. Old Paul is history. There is now a new Paul, a Paul *indwelt by Christ*. And a new Paul must have a new life. The new life that he now lived he lived "in flesh" (as a human being), but he lived it in faith, that faith of the Son of God, "Who loved me and gave Himself up for me." "Loved" is aorist tense and the aorist gathers the action in a point of time. When, in time? When our Lord handed Himself over to the death of the cross. When He gave Himself up "on behalf of" Paul, and *you*, and me.

Was this the complete end of personal sins for Paul? No. And he assumes responsibility for the sins committed by him as a believer, in Romans Seven, but he adds that it is "no longer I" but sin indwelling him. The new Paul cannot sin, but the nature of old Paul still resides in his as yet unredeemed mortal body. He, like you and I, was a saved person living in an unsaved body. He takes responsibility for his sins as a Christian, BUT recognizes the sharp cleavage that God has made between Paul, the new man and Paul the old man. "He that died has been justified from sin." Twice in Romans 7 he says, "no longer I ... but indwelling sin." Here in Galatians two it is "no longer I, but Christ indwelling me."

How can Christ dwell in a human body occupied by the old sinful nature of fallen Adam? Only with a great gulf between them!

Since you believed and God saved you, God has refused to deal with you as the fallen rebel you once were. For this reason you are now to relate to God, to "present yourself" as one "alive from the dead." "Never think of yourself apart from Christ," said John Wesley. You will have your old sin nature till Rapture or death. The war within you, with its many battles, will continue to rage this side of Heaven. Then God the Father, through God the Son, and by God the Spirit, will give you final deliverance from your "body of death."[16]

Your new nature is superior to your old nature because the new is God's answer to the old. Also because the old has only the world and the devil as allies. The new nature has God the Father, God the Son, God the Spirit, and the power of God's Word to come to its aid. "Greater is He that is in you than he that is in the world"![17] You and I are subject to defeat, but we are designed for victory. The Power who created a Universe and raised Christ from the dead lives within us![18]

The secret to success is feeding the new nature. Don't set a place at the table for the old. "Put on the Lord Jesus Christ and make NO provision for the flesh to fulfill its desires [cravings]."[19]

"Two natures dwell within my breast;
One is cursed, the other blessed.
One I love and one I hate.
The one I feed will dominate!"

You are not under Law, but under Grace. A new nature lives a new life!

CHAPTER THREE NOTES

1. Romans 8:8
2. Exodus 20:14
3. Leviticus 20:10
4. Exodus 20:13
5. Exodus 21:12
6. Romans 3:20
7. Exodus 20:1-17
8. Luke 18:13
9. Hebrews 10:10-14
10. Isaiah 64:6
11. I Timothy 1:9
12. Galatians 4:4-5
13. Colossians 3:1
14. Romans 6:9-11
15. Romans 6:12
16. Romans 7:24-25
17. I John 4:4
18. Ephesians 1:18-20
19. Romans 13:14

CHAPTER FOUR

KEYS TO BIBLE UNDERSTANDING

∽

New believers need the Word of God, and old ones as well. We need the whole Bible. We might put chocolate sprinkles on our ice cream after dinner, but the Bible is not sprinkles on our dessert. The Bible is our main course, and all that precedes a main course or follows it. It is everything from soup to nuts. "Every Scripture is God-breathed and profitable...."[1] We can never have too much doctrine (teaching material), but we can *use* too little. Many Christians seldom, if ever, *read* God's Word. Of those who do, few *study* it. Fewer still actually *believe* it. Most do not *understand* it, and almost none *apply* it. (If we didn't chew our food, digest it, and metabolize it we would die of malnutrition if starvation didn't get us first.)

I have a Chinese version of the Bible, but I can't read any of the Chinese characters. An English version that I don't understand is of no more value. There are keys to understanding the Word of God. Don't take my word for it, prove it to yourself. If someone handed you a key to your new house and on trying it you discovered that it fit the front door, the side door, the back door, the garage door, and every inside door of the house, you would realize that, in your hand you held the master key to the house. You might be given other keys that unlock one or two doors, but not all.

The master key to the Bible is something called the Mystery. There are a number of other keys each of which has its own importance. Keys to Bible understanding are not hard to come by – sometimes there may be several used in one passage.

Take I Corinthians 2:9. It says, "But as it is written, 'Eye has not seen, nor ear heard, neither have entered into the heart of man, the things which God has prepared for them that love Him.'" First, the writer – Paul – is quoting a passage from the Old Testament which he, like Christ, believes to be Scripture, or God's Word. Second, there is a line of truth which is not learned by observation, instruction, or rationale. Third, God means for a specific group of people, those who love Him, (there are those who don't), to profit from this line of truth. If we are careless students, the temptation will be to assume that the Apostle is telling us that unimaginable pleasures await our discovery in Heaven; but look at the next verse. "But God *has* revealed them unto us by His Spirit: for the Spirit searches all things, yes, the deep things of God."

Remember, keys are necessary to unlock doors – or Bible passages! And here we have a very important key, the key of *context*. Context is necessary to understanding. Cults and apostate churches frequently base a major teaching on one verse without regard for the passage surrounding it. Many *serious* errors can be avoided by looking at the preceding verse or verses, or at the succeeding verse or verses.

If we were tempted to believe that verse nine speaks of heavenly things that can't be known by those on Earth, verse ten certainly corrects that false impression. Verse ten is part of the context of verse nine, and necessary to its understanding. Verse ten shows us that the things that can't be known through our eyes, ears, or heart have already been disclosed to *us* by God. Another key to Bible understanding is found in verse ten. God reveals these otherwise unknowable things through His Spirit, and *the Spirit is a Person*, not a "force." A force cannot *search* all things, even the deep things of God. Elsewhere in Scripture, "pneuma" is used of impersonal qualities, but not here. Now we discover another key to aid us in understanding, appreciating, and even *loving* the Word of God. The key is *observing words used in apposition* (different words referring to the same person or thing). In verse nine, we have *"things"* which can only be known through divine revelation but have been prepared for "us" by God. In verse ten, these "things" are identified as the *"deep things of God"* or "God's deep things." They are "the things of God" again mentioned in verse 11, and we are told that they are, until He reveals them, known only to "the Spirit of God." So the Spirit "reveals" and "searches" (v. 10), "knows" (11), "teaches" and *"communicates"* (13). In context it is the *secret* things of man (persons) which are known only to the person himself. Non-secret things can be known by others.

I once visited a man who was dying of cancer. He told me that he could never be saved because as a young man, he had done something so terrible that God could never forgive it. He said that no one alive on Earth knew that he had done it. It was known to God alone. We opened the Bible to Romans 5 and he saw that while some might die for an upright or a good person, Christ died for the powerless, the ungodly (actively irreverent) (v.6), the sinner (v.8), those who have incurred His wrath (v.9), and His enemies (v.10). The cancer patient, George, with the "unforgivable" sin, trusted Christ who died for "unforgivable" sins, and is now in Heaven with his Savior.

There is no salvation for ladies and gentlemen, but only for sinners, enemies, objects of God's wrath. Christ has never saved one single "lady" or "gentleman," but He saves ruined, wretched sinners by the millions and saves some every hour of every day. It was for enemies – hopeless and helpless ungodly sinners, people whose deeds deserve the wrath of God – that Christ died, and not for ladies and gentlemen. Are you a sinner? Come to Christ! He may not know how to save ladies and gentlemen, but He sure knows how to save sinners. Come "hat in hand" to Calvary's cross. Come just as you are, bringing only your sins. Christ alone can save you from the wages of sin, and He would love to do it!

Not one of us can go to God and say, "See, I'm upright," or "See, I'm good." Christ wasn't sitting at a desk on Calvary, making deals with "good" people; He was hanging on a cross bearing the wrath of God for our sins, the least of which was a monstrous offense to a holy God, and enough to send us to Gehenna, the "garbage dump" of eternity. Religion may invite you to salvation as a "diamond in the rough" in need of some shaping and polishing. But we must come to Him as "garbage for the dump" and let Him create us anew in Christ. "His blood can make the foulest clean, His blood availed for me." You and I cannot bring our human righteousness to Calvary. Our relative "goodness" was not just *ignored* at Calvary, it was *rejected*. The bad news is: "Nothing less than the death of the Son of God on the cross can get a sinner into Heaven." The good news is: "Nothing more than that is needed!"

I Corinthians 2:11 teaches us that no one knows the secret things of God except God's Spirit. We believers have received God's Spirit. Why would the Third Person of the triune Godhead indwell saved sinners? "...That we might know the "things 'graced' (lit) to us by God" (v12). It is so vitally important that we come to know the secret things of God which He has granted, or"graced," to us; that God Himself has indwelt us in order to be our Teacher.

Wendell P. Loveless, "the father of Christian radio," who labored faithfully for many years at Moody Bible Institute and its flagship station WMBI, retired to Hawaii where he taught a Bible class in a Chinese Christian Church until he died at 95. Having listened to a considerable number of our tapes on the Gospel of Grace, he commented, "These truths ought to be known by every Christian in the world. Unfortunately they are known by only a few!"

The Holy Spirit is more than willing to teach them to every Christian, but He "communicates spiritual things by spiritual means" (lit. translation of verse thirteen) and this means that we all must scrap our groupthink faith in favor of Scripture as our only authority in matters of salvation, life, and ministry. Nearly all evangelicals will tell you that the Bible is their sole authority in matters of faith and practice. But when their groupthink faith is confronted by the plain meaning of Scripture they will defend their peer group's position by saying such things as: "I've always felt...; Grandfather thought...; My church teaches...; My pastor says...; Most people think...; The experts say...; Mom and Dad taught me...; Dr. So-and-so wrote in his nineteen books...."etc. That is *not* faith in God and His Word, it is faith in man and his traditions. But the Bible says, "...that your faith might *not* be in the wisdom of men, but in the power of God."[2]

The hardest thing for me to accept as an *unbeliever* was the truth that I had to come to God empty-handed because Christ, on His cross, paid my debt in full and God never collects a debt twice.

The hardest thing for me to accept as a *saint* was the truth that God wrote the Bible to be understood and that, while He might use men to teach me, He Himself must be *my sole authority!* I was given the responsibility of unlocking the little Village Baptist Church of Buffalo Grove, Illinois because our family lived closest to the building. One Sunday morning when I was the only person there, I thought, "I'm learning things from my own personal study of Romans that are not taught by the leaders of my denomination." It was a scary thought. Could I possibly be becoming a cultist? After all, wasn't my denomination the fundamentalists of the fundamentalists? How could I depart from some of their distinctions? Scary indeed. But I decided then and there that, while I would consult the written works and spoken words of others, the final authority for me would be God Himself! I remember the very spot I was standing on when I "crossed my Rubicon." It was the most difficult decision I've ever made as a Christian. Sadly, I have met very few fellow believers who have made it.

I have never turned back, because I believe it is God's revealed will that each of us make this same difficult decision. "Let God be true and every man a liar."[3] My dear new believer, (or old believer), have *you* scrapped man's traditions for God's truths? The Holy Spirit will communicate spiritual things to you by spiritual means if you will trust Him! But He will *never* contradict what He says in His Word. Actually His Word is what He uses to communicate to you and *His Word alone!*

Teaching the Roman Epistle to an adult Bible class in the Buffalo Grove church, I became convinced of the great doctrines of co-crucifixion, co-burial, and co-resurrection of the believer with Christ.

I also learned that the old nature didn't just "go away" at the moment of salvation or at any subsequent moment. Scripture convinced me that the war between flesh, with its old, fallen, Adamic nature and spirit with its new divinely produced nature continues until death or Rapture. You cannot make a Christian out of your fleshly nature. Scripture teaches that the corrupt nature keeps right on corrupting.[4] The challenge to us as believers is not to eradicate the old sin nature, nor to convert it, but to feed the new nature and refuse to provide supply lines to the old. Remember Augustine's favorite verse: "Put on the Lord Jesus Christ, and make no provision for the flesh to fulfill the lusts thereof."[5] Majoring in anything other than Christ is a form of idolatry and will guarantee our defeat. "Where your treasure is, there will your heart be also."[6] Learning from God and His Word about the two natures of the believer has been a great liberating process for me. It will be to anyone who studies and believes the passages about this great doctrine. Our divinely provided liberty in Christ is never a freedom to sin but always a liberty to serve.

Never mistake Grace for weakness, it is actually the power of God.

Another key to Bible understanding is to *consider related passages*. For example, the second chapter of I Corinthians throws light on John 16:12-15 and vice versa. Here, Christ informs the Twelve (Eleven at this time, but Twelve again by Acts 1:15-26) that He has a vitally important message for them to be delivered by the Holy Spirit in His then soon-coming future ministry. "I have yet many things to say to you, but you cannot bear them now. But when He, the Spirit of truth has come, He will guide you into all truth: for He shall not speak of Himself; but whatever He shall hear, that shall He speak: and He will show you coming things. He shall glorify me, for He shall receive of mine, and shall show it unto you. All things that the Father has are mine: therefore I said that He shall take of mine, and shall show it to you." No one but God could say this – not man nor angel! Put this passage next to I Corinthians 2:1-16 and mark the similarities.

In both passages Christ has a message for His followers not found in the Old Testament, nor in the Gospels. Christ could not deliver this message during His earthly ministry nor could even the Twelve, His "inner circle," have understood it if He had. The message contained "many things," "the *deep* things of God" which are "spiritual things" only communicated by "spiritual means" and only understood by "spiritual people." In both passages the new message is about Christ and exalts Him. Both contain new material.

Both concern "things" said to be things of God the Father, and of God the Son, and of God the Spirit. In both, the message is taught by the Holy Spirit and can only be spiritually discerned.

In John, the Spirit guides, speaks, hears and shows (lit. announces) (v. 13), and He glorifies, receives, and shows (lit. announces) (v. 14), receives, and announces (v. 15). In Corinthians, He reveals, and searches (v. 10), knows (v. 11), teaches, and communicates, (v. 13). All are activities only a person can perform.

Someone might ask, "Didn't God use Peter to divulge this new truth when the Spirit descended at Pentecost?" No. Peter himself says that his Pentecostal message was the subject of the prophets since time immemorial.[7] It is Paul's message that was "kept secret" (lit. silent) "since the world began."[8] "...which in other ages was *not* made known to the sons of men," and "which from the beginning of the world has been hidden *in God*."[9] This message was committed uniquely to Paul, taught *by* the Spirit *through* Paul, to the Twelve,[10] and difficult for Peter and the Twelve to apprehend, though they finally embraced it.[11]

All of the Bible is *for us*; the Epistles of Christ risen and glorified (a.k.a. the Pauline Epistles) are *to us* and *about us*. Their subject is the Mystery (secret) of uncompromised Grace, which can only be communicated *by* the Holy Spirit *to* the spiritual person.

CHAPTER FOUR NOTES

1. II Timothy 3:16
2. I Corinthians 2:5
3. Romans 3:4
4. Ephesians 4:22-24
5. Romans 13:14
6. Matthew 6:21
7. Acts 3:24
8. Romans 16:25
9. Ephesians 3:5
10. Ephesians 3:9
11. II Peter 3:15-18

CHAPTER FIVE

SIN IN THE LIFE OF THE BELIEVER

∽

Galatians 2:20 says, "I am crucified with Christ: nevertheless I live; yet not I but Christ liveth in me: and the life which I now live in the flesh I live by the faith of the Son of God, who loved me, and gave Himself for me."

Christ is more than a Jewish carpenter or a philosopher. He is uniquely infinite God and perfect Man in one Person.[1] As God, John says that He created the Universe with its trillions of stars. And He became man, without ceasing to be God. He walked among us for a third of a century with His face set as a flint toward Calvary where He died for a race of enemies.[2]

"Christ lives in me." Can this be? Is it possible that Almighty God, as Jesus Christ, actually lived in the Apostle Paul and is willing to live in you and me? Is the real secret of the Christian life "the power of Christ within"? The Bible teaches, and I believe, that this is true. The Christian life is never the result of the believer's struggle, stress, and strain. It is not a product of human effort but of the divine provision of the indwelling Christ. Christ within can mean the difference between a lifetime of success and a lifetime of failure.

All Christians fail some of the time, many much of the time, and some all of the time. Did God intend it to be so? Is it not both Scriptural and logical to believe that God would make a perfect provision for a life characterized by victory? Not a perfectly sinless life; that is impossible this side of Heaven. But a life of constant growth and increasing occupation with Christ. If success comes from consistently allowing God to live His life in and through me, then His presence should become increasingly evident to me and to others.

There is a vast difference between a believer living a moral life characterized by Christian virtues and a believer living the Spiritual life. Many good things such as zeal, compassion, industry, sacrifice, and even dedication can be mistaken for the life of Christ within revealing itself outwardly.

"Walk by the Spirit, and you shall not fulfill the lust of the flesh."[3] Some versions of the Bible say, "Walk *in* the Spirit." This assumes the dative form of pneuma, or spirit, to be locative of sphere. "Walk in the sphere of the Spirit." I have viewed it as instrumental of means. "Walk *by means of* the Spirit." The original Greek will allow either. It is also true that to walk in the sphere, or realm, of the Spirit, one would have to walk by spiritual means, while to walk by means of the Spirit one would have to walk in the realm of the Spirit. The difference is not of great consequence – certainly not one to fight over. I lean toward "by means of" because of context. "Walk" is present tense, "Keep on walking," or "Continually walk." We are told by God that this is not a temporary injunction but permanent; not something we are to do sporadically, but for a lifetime.

We must make up our minds, once and for all to "keep on walking in the realm of the Spirit and by means of the Spirit" because this is God's way for us to conduct our lives. God's *only* way. It is either God's way or the way of the flesh. There is no third way, no other option. Actually, the choice is plain: to walk spiritually, or to fulfill fleshly cravings. When I am not "walking" I am "fulfilling," whether for a minute, a day, or a lifetime.

The flesh does not always choose immoral behavior. Sometimes the flesh decides for religiosity. Religiosity, despite its repeated demands, is much easier than true spirituality. I can even be a devout evangelical without being a devout follower of Christ. Evangelicalism can take the place in my life that belongs only to Christ. I then become an evangelical idolater, and my family, my friends, and my church may not know the difference. Integrity is never devoid of morality but morality is often devoid of integrity. If you are satisfied to be active, concerned, reliable, generous, and blameless but have no hunger for the living Word and the written Word you may even fool yourself, but God is not mocked.

When, as a young and new believer, I discovered that, though much in my life had changed radically, I still sinned, I began to fear that I had lost salvation. A salvation that could be lost would not be salvation at all; it would be probation. Some indeed teach that salvation can be lost by starting to sin or ceasing to believe, but Christ did not die to be anyone's probation officer. He died to be our Savior. If you are on probation, you are *not* saved, and if you are saved you are *not* on probation. Christ died on account of our sins and was raised on account of our justification. Christ can never die again. He died once and for all. He cannot go back to the other side of Calvary and the empty tomb! Nor can you! God Himself tells us that Christ died once and forever and that He now lives unto God. Then God tells us that we are to reckon, or acknowledge ourselves to have died with Him – once forever, and to be *really* dead to sin and alive to God, as is Christ.[4]

What about my "today" sins then? What about the things I think that a believer shouldn't think, the things I say that I shouldn't say, the things I do that I shouldn't do? How should I view them? I should view them as things that displease God, for God is never pleased with sin. But I should also view them as died for by Christ and forgiven by God, and removed forever. That God has not only erased Heaven's blackboard, but thrown the blackboard away should cause me to know Him better, enable me to love Him more, and compel me to serve Him always. If the Grace of God does not so move me, nothing will, not fear of punishment nor hope of reward.

There is no understanding of the Christian life without an understanding of the fullness and finality of the believer's co-death, co-burial, and co-resurrection with Christ. This operation of God is said in Scripture to be for every believer and to have culminated in our present seating with Christ in the heavenly places. That Christ is permanently seated at the right hand of the Father *right now* is a tremendously meaningful truth.[5] That you and I are seated with Him, presently and permanently is its companion truth.[6] We have every bit as much reason to believe the second truth as to believe the first.

"I am crucified with Christ." "I am crucified" is perfect tense. The perfect tense always refers to an action completed in time past with ongoing, or continuing results. To do justice to the original Greek, one would have to say, "I have been completely crucified with Christ in time past with the present result that I am still completely crucified." Companion passages show our co-crucifixion to be complete and permanent.

The phrase "with Christ" clearly demonstrates that this is not an experience to be sought by the believer in his own lifetime, but something that God did for him in the first century. The Bible teaches that Christ could only be crucified once and that His crucifixion took place in the first century A.D. Many have taught that the believer is to crucify himself or to be crucified subsequent to personal salvation. But this would require Christ to be crucified with us in our century, which is utterly impossible. He cannot be crucified again. Moreover, we are said to have been crucified *with Him*, not He with us!

How could we be crucified centuries before we were born? Because *His death* was *our death*; He had no death of His own to die. Death had absolutely no claim on Him; death is the wages of sin, and *He had no sin*. A death, in full payment of the wages of sin, was died *by Christ* for us, and in that sense *we died with Him*!

Since God never collects a debt twice, and He collected my debt at Calvary, sin is no longer an issue. It is no longer able to separate me from God.

"Nevertheless I live." Old Paul was crucified; new Paul lives. Old Paul, under condemnation, had to be crucified before new Paul, uncondemned, could live. And so it is with us – with you and with me. Our life in sin, under condemnation, and facing judgment had to end forever for life under Grace to begin!

Religion hates revelation, have you discovered this? Man's traditions will always oppose God's truth. The natural (lit. "soulish") man *cannot* understand Grace. Period. The natural man, the unsaved man, the once-born man may rise to the heights in religion but "that which has been [perfect tense] born of the flesh is [continues to be, present tense, linear action] flesh." Flesh never becomes spirit, it remains flesh, permanently flesh, forever flesh, and that is the bad news. The good news is "that which has been born [perfect tense] of the Spirit, is [continues to be, present tense, linear action] spirit." And that is why our Adamic "flesh" *nature* had to die that our new Christian *nature* could replace it. Our *legal union* with Adam had to end so that a new and permanent *legal union* with Christ could begin. "No longer I, but Christ lives in me." Twice in Romans 7, Paul says, "No longer I...but sin dwelling in me." The problem is indwelling sin; the solution is the indwelling Christ. Christ within will always triumph over sin within if we obey the Scripture: "But put on the Lord Jesus Christ and make no provision for the flesh, to fulfill the lusts thereof." Sin is powerful, but it must be provided for. Sin is powerful, but its supply lines can be cut.

What you do when you realize that you have sinned reveals how much you grasp of the Grace of God. Paul acknowledges his sins and makes no attempt to deny responsibility for them in Romans 7. But he distinguishes between himself and his old sin nature. (There are three "I's" in the chapter: the old I, the responsible I, and the new I.) Sin cannot be charged to the new Paul because "that which has been born of God does not sin." In Romans 8, God Himself cannot charge the twice-born man with sin, having Himself justified him and declared him righteous. Christ Himself cannot condemn him, having died in his place. You will never hear these consequences of our union with Christ in His crucifixion, death, burial, and resurrection taught by Religion though they are self-evident truths plainly stated in God's Word. Religion is threatened by Grace. Religion opposes Grace. Religion cannot grasp Grace. Religion has NO Savior!

Sins in the life of the believer are never the will of God. But we *do* sin because we have a sin nature. The challenge is not to eradicate the old sinful nature – that cannot be done. The challenge is not to live a completely sin-free life – that cannot be done either. The challenge is to learn to live increasingly in the new nature – to "put on Christ." We ought to be more successful in responding to life in our new nature this year than last, this month than last, and this week than last week.

We need to pray daily that Christ's love of righteousness and His hatred of sin will become ours. "It is God who works in you both to will and to do of His good pleasure."

Are you learning to love God, His Word, and His will more and more?

CHAPTER FIVE NOTES

1. John 1:1,14
2. Romans 5:10
3. Galatians 5:16
4. Romans 6:10-11
5. Hebrews 1:3
6. Ephesians 2:4-6

CHAPTER SIX

FEEDING THE NEW DOG

Life is far more difficult for some people than it is for others. I once augmented my income by driving a small bus full of blind teens to summer day camp. Most of them were twins. They were born prematurely and the custom at the time was to put them in oxygen chambers to assist their underdeveloped lungs. Too much oxygen caused blindness, usually in the smaller twin, sometimes in both. Life for them was far more difficult – from the cradle to the grave – than for children born with eyesight. A child born in the third world, or with a crippling disease, or to abusive parents has a much steeper hill to climb than those more fortunate.

One Christian's life may be vastly more difficult than that of others too, but the *degree of difficulty* is not the issue for us who know the Lord. The issue is always the *extent of supply*. Your life may be one that is extremely hard, but God has made a perfect provision for *every* believer to survive – even to triumph! Take heart; God is infinitely bigger than any of our challenges. Peter says, "Casting all your care upon Him, because He cares for you."[1]

Francis of Assisi prayed, "God grant me the Serenity to accept the things I cannot change, the Courage to change the things I can, and the Wisdom to know the difference." It is a prayer I pray frequently.

There are some very practical things that you can do to radically change the quality of your life and ministry.

STUDY! The believer's *first* priority is Bible study: the regular intake of sound Bible doctrine. This is not possible in most of the countries on this planet because the "god" of this world establishes his dictatorial control of governments and their societies wherever and as soon as he can. Just owning a Bible is a felony in much of the world. But if you *can* study, you should. No, if you *can*, you MUST! God calls every believer to study the Bible. Think of yourself as someone on a mission, because that's who you are. An emissary of Heaven on loan to planet Earth. Each born again Christian actually belongs to God.[2] We are His properties even if and when we are not acting as if we were. Our minds are His, and our bodies too! We steal our minds and bodies from their true Owner. We go through life in possession of stolen property and never even think of ourselves as thieves.

We are here, not to be happy, healthy, and wealthy – though all of these are good, but to do those things that please *our Father. We cannot do the will of God until we know the will of God, and we cannot* know the will of God except through Scripture. By the will of God, I do not mean whom or whether to marry, what vocation to pursue, in what place to reside, or whether to buy the large white two-story on the hill or the little green bungalow in the valley. God's will is everywhere in Scripture. We don't need a "still, small voice" to whisper to us while we shower; we need to studiously apply ourselves to the daily study of His Book.

Briefly stated, God's will is that we, you and I, "present [ourselves] to God as living sacrifices."[3] The verb "to present" is in the aorist tense; all the action is gathered in a point in time. It is punctiliar. Do it now! It is the decisive, well-considered, joyful, eager adoption of my lifetime attitude. The adjective "living" is in the present tense, with linear or on-going action. It is the lifetime, consistent, determined living out of my God-given attitude. Nothing more than being a "living sacrifice" is possible. Nothing less is worship and service. Until you and I declare ourselves to be wholly God's, and at His disposal, *we have not worshipped.*

For 19 years, we had a radio program. Thousands called or wrote us. Many expressed an interest in attending our Grace Fellowship. It was not uncommon for a caller to ask, "Do you worship?" Usually they meant, "Do you sing, etc.?" Singing, etc., *can* be an *expression* of worship, but it is not in itself worship. Worship is always the daily living out of a conscious decision to be His in a very practical sense, and to live 24 hours a day as if we were.

I do not agree with some of John Wesley's doctrine but I would stand at attention and remove my hat if he passed by. You cannot read a biography of the man and come away doubting that all of him was on the altar. Or David Livingstone. Maybe he was hard to get along with at times, but he was sold out to the principle that the very breath in our nostrils is God's – and every last heartbeat. Or Fanny Crosby, who never let her lifelong blindness and poor health diminish her passion to honor and serve Christ. Or C.T. Studd, who gladly scrapped wealth and fame to "burn out" for His Lord. It was Studd who said, "If Jesus Christ be God and died for me, then *no* sacrifice can be too great for me to make for Him."

It's easy for someone, looking for the First Church of Fun and Games to inquire, "Do you worship?" We *all* need to ask ourselves, "Do I live daily, even hourly, as a total, once-for-ever sacrifice?" English translators ask us to "yield" ourselves. God says "Present yourself!" There is a significant difference. "Yield" is an Islamic concept. A wrestler may yield reluctantly but it is impossible to *present* reluctantly – it cannot be done other than joyfully. The military command to "Present arms!" is a symbolic call to willingly present your rifle – and everything it represents – to a cause you believe in and a country you love? I can yield to a "god" quite against my will, to a "god" who is bigger and meaner than I, to save my skin. I can only eagerly present all that I am or ever hope to be to a God with whom I am having a divine "love affair"!

The foundation of practical Christianity is always positional Christianity. "I am who I am so I do what I do." God always tells you what He has made Christ to be to you, and who He has made you to be in Christ, and *THEN* He appeals to you to act accordingly.

"Doctrine is the stuff that life is made of!" You can never have too much of it, but you *can* use too little. God employed our Apostle, Paul, to lay the foundation. The superstructure, walls and roof must agree with the foundation.

You may not have acquired a hunger for God's Word. Perhaps you can't say, "Thy words were found and I did eat them, and Thy Word was to me the joy and rejoicing of my heart."[4] Pray until you can! Daily. Hourly. Never settle for less than a constant hunger for God's Word. Your love for the Bible will always reflect your love for God, and vice versa. You will never say truthfully, "As the deer pants for the water brooks, my heart pants for you,"[5] until God's Word is the consuming passion of your very soul.

There is a chapter in this book dedicated to the subject of prayer. However, you will live and die with unanswered questions about prayer. So will I. Prayer has more than its share of mystery. But there is much that we *can know, and must know*, that we can learn from Bible study. The rest we must leave to God. God calls us to pray.

I knew a man from Zion, Illinois who was one of the most dedicated soul winners I have ever met. His wife laughingly complained to me that if she turned her head to ask him a question in a supermarket aisle, more often than not, he wouldn't be there. She said she would likely find him outside witnessing to a group of teenagers or to the policeman on the corner. Harold travelled all over the world on business. He always testified of Christ to the person in the next seat and frequently the Holy Spirit would lead the person to Christ before the plane landed, or the train pulled into the station. Once in Chicago, he was passing out tracts from car to car on the elevated. He gave one to a girl reading a Bible, and was delighted to learn that she was a believer – and that she was my bride. But Harold, who taught me so much by the life that he lived, once confessed to me, "Jim, I never pray. It may be wrong, but I never pray."

I haven't figured that one out yet. It is a most natural thing to speak to those we love. The God who makes us "fishers of men" is the same God who says, "Men ought *always* to pray, and not to faint" (to lose heart)."[6] Prayer is not just "asking and receiving" although it certainly includes that. Prayer is a form of worship, and God is seeking true worshippers.[7] Prayer should be a continued indication of our complete and unending dependence upon Him. God does not need our prayers – we need them.

About three months after I assumed my second, (and last) pastorate, a young man came to me and, after thanking me for answering so many of his questions in a very short time, he said, "But I have one problem...." "I know, it's prayer." Surprised, he asked how I knew. "When people begin to understand the Dispensation of Grace (a.k.a. the Church era) and Grace itself, they always have trouble with the traditional views of prayer. He said that he only prayed about 10% as much as he had before he knew what promises belong to the Body of Christ and which don't. "Yes," said my wife, "but your prayers are probably 90% more Scriptural."

To pray "in Jesus' name" means on Jesus' authority. One can't approach God for something He hasn't promised to give and do it "on Jesus' authority." I pray about, and sometimes for, things that are not guaranteed to today's believer by the Word, but it would be inappropriate to claim our Lord's authority for it. For instance, I know that God wants me to study and learn from Scripture, to avoid sexual immorality, to love my enemies, to be kind; God's will on those things – and many more – is clearly revealed in His Word. So, when I pray for His help in doing His will I can make my requests "in Jesus' name"or "on the authority of Christ." I might pray to God to keep my grandmother safe on her motorcycle. I think I would, especially if she's entered in the 100 mile national championship race at Laconia, but I wouldn't pray as Christ's representative. By the way, God never tells us to *say* "in Jesus' name," but just to "*pray* in His name." No prayer in the Bible ends with those words. But many Christians think God won't hear and answer unless they use these three little words as a rabbit's foot, a magic talisman, an "open sesame."

Once, in my college days at Barrington, I was invited by a classmate to an all-night prayer meeting that he had arranged. It began at 7 p.m. By nine, 15 of the 20 or so people had left. By 10:30, only my classmate and I remained. "This isn't working," he commented. At 11:30, he turned to me and said, "Well, we've prayed for quite a while, why don't we call it quits?" Was I relieved! Not only had I been fighting sleep for an hour, but I was the last to leave. I think that I fairly oozed spiritual pride. Well, would you believe carnal pride?

I used to feel like God's worst investment, a total write-off, when I would read that Wesley prayed three hours a day, Luther four, and Praying Hyde for eight. A day characterized by "sentence prayers" can be well spent. If you start with sentence prayers, as a new believer, you will find out two things: some of your sentence prayers will become paragraphs and, before long, chapters. And an hour without prayer will feel like an hour stolen by the sin nature (which it is).

Major in Bible study and prayer. It shouldn't affect you that most others don't, and don't become prideful. "What do you have that you didn't receive?" Christ prayed all night sometimes. Perhaps, you shall too. I don't, but I begin each bedtime with prayer and often pray at times during the night. Kneeling seems to make me sleepy automatically. Once I saw a priest praying while walking in a courtyard. I copied him and have done most of my concentrated praying while pacing ever since.

Sentence prayers are great while driving – just don't close your eyes! There is a time to get alone and concentrate on talking to the Father, and on nothing else, but sentence prayers are good most any time. A friend heard me talk about sentence prayers. The next morning he prayed briefly as soon as he sat in his car. In the roofing business, he does quite a bit of driving. Now, driving for him means praying as well. Habit can be a great thing. Good habits can be strong influences in the believer's life. My friend, the roofer, became so excited about his new found prayer life that he made a study of the prayers of Paul and wrote a booklet on the subject.

When Bible study and prayer have become staples, add witnessing. Personal evangelism can be a most challenging ministry, but God has called *all* believers to do it. Don't shun things simply because they are difficult. Call on God for courage and "spiritual tact." Winning souls is not learned by reading books. Like flying airplanes, it is learned "in the doing" of it. Don't shrink from making mistakes. Everyone makes them. Try not to repeat them. Stick with your God-ordained and God-enabled ministry until it becomes more natural to speak to others about their salvation than not to do it. The best personal evangelism flows from the believer's excitement over the Person and work of Christ.

Constant Bible study, constant prayer, and constant personal work witnessing to the unsaved about "the grace of God that brings salvation"[8] and to the saved about "the grace of God that is able to build you up"[9] are all part of a healthy spiritual life. *Believers who are serious about God, and Christ, and the Bible, and other Christians are seldom depressed.* Mental health facilities are full of professing Christians who suffer from severe emotional upset, and even mental illness. I have yet to find one believer in a psyche ward who consistently follows the practical instructions God gives us in the "owner's manual." Healthy worship and service produces healthy living.

Learn early that your physical health, wealth, and happiness are not really what life is all about. Only Christ matters! When these three words truly become yours, your life and ministry will be characterized by triumph, and not just by survival.

You belong in the best gospel preaching assembly you can find. Most of the saints in this world have no assembly, and many are not able to "attend" by TV or radio. But if you live near a gospel preaching assembly, then attendance is not an option. God's will is plain and inescapable. "Not forsaking the assembling of ourselves together."[10]

God designed the true Bible "church" and supplied the gift, the office of pastor-teacher, to bring us, one and all, to maturity.[11] The textbook is the Word of God, rightly divided.[12] Our major is the study of the Person and work of Christ. "Till we all arrive at the unity of the faith, and of the advanced knowledge of the Son of God, at a man full grown...." You're not there yet. You don't have your doctorate in the advanced knowledge of Jesus Christ. Neither do I. So we'd better fall in with God's plan for our education – the local assembly – and stay with the plan till death or Rapture.

And don't be a bump on a log. Find something that needs doing that you can do, and *do it* in and through your local assembly. Glorify God in your body and spirit. You *belong* to Him!

CHAPTER SIX NOTES

1. I Peter 5:7
2. I Corinthians 6:19-20
3. Romans 12:1-2
4. Jeremiah 15:16
5. Psalm 42:1
6. Luke 18:1
7. John 4:23
8. Titus 2:11
9. Acts 20:32
10. Hebrews 10:25
11. Ephesians 4:11-16
12. II Timothy 2:15

CHAPTER SEVEN

WHY US?

~

The original book and the original movie called *Zulu*, were taken from an actual historical incident. The Zulus began as a tribe, a single ethnicity. A great warrior people, they soon conquered a number of hostile tribes and incorporated them into the Zulu nation. They were joined by other friendly tribes seeking protection or fearing destruction. From the family came the tribe, the nation, and finally, the empire. The Zulus had not only a great military, but an outstanding civilization. The Dutch, who occupied South Africa before the coming of the Zulus, and the English who came afterward, clashed with the Zulus and the Zulus with them.

Zulu, the book become movie, is about a company of Welsh regulars in the British Army who "holed up" in a mission compound when cornered by 4,000 battle-hardened Zulu tribesmen. The tribesmen, after several assaults and much hard fighting costly to both sides, on the verge of victory over the Welsh company, suddenly withdrew from the field of battle in respect for and as a salute to the courage of the Brits. Seventeen Brits won Victoria crosses that day – Britain's highest decoration – something unheard of in British history. There were many Zulu heroes, too.

Just before the conflict, the Welsh detachment heard a noise like the noise of a great freight train approaching, but there were no trains there in the desert. Instead it was the sound of over 4,000 Zulus rhythmically beating spears against shields which they did to announce their coming and to strike fear into the hearts of the foe. Realizing what logic demanded would be the outcome of this battle, one young private tearfully asked his sergeant, "Why us?" "Because we're here, son, because we're here," was his Sergeant's reply.

"We're here," too, you and I. From the moment of our salvation we have been citizens of Heaven. We don't belong "here." We belong "there"! But we're here, so "It's us or rust!" God has not given the priceless privilege of bragging about Christ to angels. Not even to supermen. But to us. And we have just one brief lifetime to get it done!

> "Only one life, 'twill soon be past,
> Only what's done for Christ will last."

Know who you are! You started life as fallen Adam's fallen progeny. As a sinner by nature, by choice, by practice and by divine indictment. In sin, under condemnation, hell-bound, and hell-deserving. Garbage for the dump!

When Grace found you, God wrought His greatest miracle. Grace broke your bond to fallen Adam and united you completely and eternally to your new Federal Head, Christ. "If anyone be in Christ, he is a new creation. Old things [sin, condemnation, fallenness, eternal loss – all] have passed away. All things have become new."[1]

Since you came empty-handed to the cross, you have been a totally new creation: equipped for Earth, but designed for Heaven; equipped for time, but designed for eternity.[2]

You have two natures: the one bequeathed to you by fallen Adam, the other created for you by Christ. You are now a walking contradiction. One third of your being loves Christ and wants to serve Him; one third loves self and wants to serve it; and one third (one very mysterious third) decides whether to respond to God, to life, to self, and to others in the new nature or the old.

Success is not making a Christian of your old nature, that's impossible; it is responding increasingly to life's challenges in the new nature. Are you more successful at doing this *now* than *then*?

Know why you're here. Much of today's "evangelism" would lead us to believe that "The chief end of man is to acquire health, wealth, and happiness. If you don't have all three, you're a loser, but take heart. God is on your side and, if you follow a few simple steps, you can be a winner. God can't wait to increase your happiness quotient." But "The chief end [purpose] of man is [still] to glorify God and enjoy Him forever."[3] These goals are poles apart and "never the twain shall meet"! The "health, wealth, and happiness" movement is based on self-worship – essentially idolatry. Textbooks say that idolatry began with Nimrod. I don't think so. It began in Adam's garden, with Satan, Eve, and Adam. Satan said to Eve, "You shall be as gods," and he has been saying this to Adam's race ever since. All idolatry is man's worship of himself, in the final analysis.

You are here as God's creation – a sort of first fruit of the new creation. You are a new creation being living in the old creation. A saved person in an unsaved body. A pilgrim. Well, Pilgrim, "this world is not [our] home, [we're] just a passin' through." That's what pilgrims do, Pilgrim, they just pass through. Don't get too comfortable here in Vanity Fair. "Here" is not permanent; "there" is permanent. You can't take it with you. None of it. So, don't hold any of what's here too closely.

Dottie Rambo, the songwriter, wrote:

> "The things that I love, and hold dear to my heart
> are just borrowed, they're not mine at all;
> Jesus only let me use them to brighten my life.
> So, remind me, remind me, dear Lord."

If your treasure is here on Earth, get ready. Moth, rust, and thieves are on their way. Your treasure must be Christ. He must come before everything and everyone. When anything or anyone comes before Christ in your life, you are not operating as God designed you to operate.

It is a wonderful thing to love your parents, your siblings, your spouse, your children, and so on. It is good for you to love all of these and more. But one of Satan's specialties is turning good things into bad. If he can't get you to hate people, he will get you to love them more than your Creator/Savior. Loving people doesn't cause us to love God. Loving God causes us to love people. Loving people is God's will for every believer. But, putting *anyone* where only Christ belongs is idolatry and idolatry is always sin. *Terrible* sin!

We were made "*by* Him [Christ] and *for* Him." If we wish to be successful at life and ministry we must become, and remain, occupied with Christ. True happiness always comes from being in the center of God's will. True happiness is the result of the believer's integrity. There is *no* integrity outside of the will of God. There is no integrity without occupation with Christ. Satan offers many substitutes. Occupation with ministry is a subtle substitute. Occupation with sex is a more obvious one. If the enemy cannot destroy you through illicit sex, he may seek to destroy you through the success of your ministry. And every believer has one or more ministries, whether fulfilled or unfulfilled. Christian life brings with it responsibility. Grace made Paul a debtor to all, and you as much as Paul!

I knew a couple who attended church faithfully, supported it generously, and worked in it steadily. Would to God that all believers had this resume. But neither *ever* shared the plan of salvation with their parents, and both sets of parents died unsaved. These two are to be commended for their loyalty, sacrifice, industry, and zeal. They are to be indicted for wasting years of opportunity to win Mom and Dad to Christ. Their negligence, born of the fear of rejection, showed an awful lack of love for their respective parents – and a lack of love for Christ.

But if Satan can't scare you out of witnessing, he'll get you to love personal Christian work more than you love Christ. Personal evangelism should become a habit, then an addiction, then an obsession, but never a source of pride, and never an idol.

"You shall worship the Lord, your God and Him *only* shall you serve."[4] Service does not guarantee worship; worship inclines us to serve. But service must *always* have its roots down deep into worship. Without a life of worship, service becomes a mechanical counterfeit, a salve for our guilt, and a boon to our ego.

Have you ever thought of this? From the moment you set foot on Heaven's beach, you will serve God perfectly and eternally. But you and I will never again have the opportunity to serve Him in Satan's world, among hostile people, in an evil age, in a difficult time, surrounded by conflict, and indwelt by fears. What a challenge!

I wonder if one day's service on Earth won't outshine an aeon of service in Heaven! Could the greatest gift we could ever present to our Savior in eternity be ourselves on the altar of time? "Redeeming the time, because the days are evil."[5] Buy up each opportunity to serve, while the opportunities are available.

"For we are His workmanship, created in Christ Jesus *for good works*, which God previously planned that *we should walk in their sphere.*"[6]

Serving our Lord is the highest privilege available to created beings, angelic or human. When service becomes a chore it ceases to be service. We *cannot* serve God to escape getting a flat tire on a country road in a rainstorm at night. Nor can we serve Him to earn a larger house on a wider street in Heaven. If what we do is motivated by either the carrot or the stick, we are actually serving ourselves and our own best interests and not serving Him at all.

Have you learned to experience the sheer joy of being a "nothing" that God can use?

CHAPTER SEVEN NOTES

1. II Corinthians 5:17
2. II Corinthians 5:1-8
3. Westminster Shorter Catechism
4. Matthew 4:10
5. Ephesians 5:16
6. Ephesians 2:10

CHAPTER EIGHT

STANDING AND STATE

One very simple key to understanding the Bible and to understanding ourselves, for that matter, is the doctrine, or teaching, that distinguishes "standing" from "state."

Standing is what God has made us to be in Christ. State is what we're doing with standing. Standing is just that, our standing before a thrice-holy God, "dressed in His righteousness *alone, faultless* to stand before the throne." We stand in Grace, therefore our standing never changes – not by a nickel's worth. We can't lose it by being bad, because we didn't get it by being good. "God justifies [declares righteous] the ungodly."[1] And, having a relationship with God that can never be altered, diminished, or revoked should make us want to be holy – to "do always those things that please Him." Grace is never an incitement to sin; it is always an inducement to serve. It makes good Christians better and bad Christians good.

Years ago, I was riding on a bus in Chicago and reading a paperback by Walter Wilson, M.D., the physician turned Bible teacher. Dr. Wilson said that no man could possibly stand before God in his own human righteousness, and no man could fail to stand before God in the righteousness of God. Instantly, the whole thrust of the book of Romans came together in my head. I had been a Christian for ten years; now, for the first time, I *knew* that my salvation made me eternally secure. Before that, I had been "proof-texted" into "believing" in eternal security and "proof-texted" out of "believing" in it a hundred times. Now I had something more than proof-texts. I had a concept, one that permeates the entire Bible, but is clearly revealed in those books written to and about "the church, which is His body."[2] These books that should be labeled "The message of Christ, Risen and Glorified" and only sub-titled "The Pauline Epistles." And the concept is this: Human righteousness *cannot* bring man eternal life. On his best day, a man's own personal righteousness is "filthy rags" in the sight of God.[3] Your righteous acts and mine – the best things that could ever be said about us – were not only ignored at Calvary, they were *rejected*! Calvary is God's repudiation of man's goodness! "If righteousness comes through Law, then *CHRIST DIED FOR NOTHING!* "[4]

Romans five shows us that Christ did not die for ladies and gentlemen; He wouldn't know how to do that. Christ died for sinful, rebellious, enemies. Hell-bound, hell-deserving wretches. If you came to Christ as a "diamond in the rough," YOU ARE NOT SAVED. The saved brought nothing to Calvary but their sins. We came as "garbage for the dump." Any dignity we have came to us by Grace alone. Our worth can only be attributed to Christ's death for us on His cross. Our sins, His cross! We must *never* forget it. He paid the highest price that will ever be paid for anything when He redeemed us through His substitutionary death, and that gave us all the dignity we will ever need or can ever have.

When men intrude man's imagined righteousness into God's plan of salvation, Grace becomes non-Grace and non-Grace is anti-Grace. Adding human merit to God's pure Grace (could Grace be less than pure?), is like adding anthrax to pumpkin pie.

If you think you were saved by making some "commitment" or other to God, think again. Study what the Bible says about salvation. Your fingerprints are nowhere to be found on your salvation. Salvation is wholly a work of God for the sinner, and NEVER the sinner's work for God, in whole or in part. In Scripture, Christ, who is God, does ALL the saving; and you and I do only all the being saved. We believe; God saves. Thus be it ever! God performs ALL of the action in the verb "to save." We sinners receive the action of the verb.

No one has ever received God's gift of eternal life by "giving his heart to Jesus," "making a commitment of his life to God," "giving his heart to God," or "doing" anything at all. Believing is the only thing that we can "do" without "doing" anything. Christ was not sitting at a desk on Calvary receiving *anything* from man. He was hanging on a cruel and criminal cross giving His everything to totally ruined wretches. You can't come to Christ as an NFL quarterback or a Miss America. Jesus' blood can make the vilest sinner clean. It does nothing for Hall of Famers or beauty pageant winners. "It saved the worst among you, when it saved a wretch like me."

You can throw game-winning passes until you wear SuperBowl rings on all your fingers and toes, but you still have to be saved like the thief on the cross. I've pointed out to dozens of priests that the thief on the cross only believed and was saved without doing one work. The thief was spiked to that cross; he couldn't come down and help one senior carry one bag of groceries. The priests, Catholic, Protestant, Orthodox and otherwise all say, "The thief on the cross was an exception." Oh, no he wasn't! He was the rule. Salvation must come to you as it did to him – by Grace alone!

On Calvary, Christ, with every last one of our filthy, wretched, foul, rotten sins upon Him, was forsaken by God and man. "He [Christ] BY HIMSELF PURGED OUR SINS,"[5] and He purged ALL of them – the ones we brag about to our friends and the ones we wouldn't want Mother to know. NOWHERE IN SCRIPTURE does Christ die for some of our sins, our past sins only, our "little" sins, or "understandable" sins. EVERYWHERE IN SCRIPTURE He dies for all of our sins – every single one. Our big ones as well as the small, oft-repeated sins as well as single "mistakes," our sinful habits, addictions, compulsions, and yes, even our *sinful nature* that produces our sins. Tomorrow's sins as well as yesterday's! They were ALL tomorrow's sins when Christ went to the cross for them.

And He went to the cross *alone*! According to God, and Christ, and the Bible, Christ had no helpers. No Protestant, Catholic, Orthodox, or other helpers. Salvation, whether viewed as Redemption, Reconciliation, Justification, Propitiation, Regeneration, Forgiveness, or any of the other 36 values of the cross, is ALWAYS and ONLY attributed to Christ alone! Never to Christ plus Mary, the martyrs, the saints, the "sacraments," any church, priesthood, rite, or ritual. CHRIST ALONE! Do we get it? Do we get it? CHRIST ALONE!

If what God says in His Word is not good enough for you, your umbilical cord must be plugged into "groupthink" and not Scripture. CUT THE CORD!

Now, back to standing and state. When you were saved, your new birth gave you a new nature, making you part of the new creation. The Bible speaks of a day when Christ will "make all things new;"[6] when He will roll up the entire Universe with its trillions of stars, lay it all aside like a discarded garment, and create a wholly new Universe.[7] You are a part of that new creation ALREADY![8] Do you know that? Do you believe it? If God is saying that to us right now through His Word, the Bible, we *can* believe it and *must*. Imagine that! Go look at yourself in the mirror and tell yourself, "Honey, you don't look like much now, but you're actually already part of the New Heavens and the New Earth."[9] A kind of "first-fruit" of eternity future.

If you've trusted Christ as your complete and only Savior, Heaven is yours, and you can never lose it, because of your standing, your position. You stand! You stand before God in your eternal union with Christ. You can never lose your perfect position before God, because neither Satan with all his power and craft, nor you and I with all our sinfulness and stupidity can undo the crosswork of Christ. What God has done cannot be undone by angels or man.

> "Near, so very near to God,
> Nearer I could not be;
> For, in the Person of His Son
> I am as near as He."

That's your position, your standing. Has your church told you that? Your Bible has, and will continue to if you'll let it.

But, if my standing is my new and permanent, even eternal position before God, as inviolate and unchangeable as God Himself, what is my state? Your state is your spiritual "batting average," and it can change from day to day, even from moment to moment. Your standing is a work of God. Your state is what you are doing with your standing. God the Father holds us in His clenched fist. God the Son holds us in His clenched fist. English versions may say, "...'no *man*' " can wrench us from God's grasp,"[10] but the Greek in which

God wrote John ten, (God never wrote a word in English), says "... no *one* can snatch us from that grasp." "No one" is wider than "no man." No one includes angels as well as humans. Even Satan. No one, not Satan himself, can wrest you from the fist of God! That's standing, Brother! That's standing, Sister!

The short term news about state is not as good, but it's still good. God has made a perfect provision for every believer's state. One day, in Heaven, our state will match our standing. We shall then be able to say what only Christ could say, "I do always those things that please Him." We can't *say* that now, because we can't *do* that now. Though God has made a perfect provision for each of us to be winners in our war with indwelling sin, He hasn't made our mortality into immortality yet. We still live as "saved people in unsaved bodies;" nor has He "made corruption into incorruptibility."[11] But sin is never God's will for the believer. And we can never excuse giving in to indwelling sin and letting it "reign as king in [our] mortal body."[12] Thank God, the sin nature cannot reign in our spirit, in our new man, just in our body. Thank God, too, that the sin nature's reign positionally has been broken and that its power in our walk can be broken too!

Our original progenitor, unfallen Adam, was *designed* to live in total dependence upon God. He rebelled against his Creator, choosing independence and plunging Adam the individual, and Adam the race into a helpless and hopelessly lost condition. That's where you were when Grace found and saved you – helpless and hopeless! "The Son of Man came to seek and to save that which was lost."[13] He seeks all men, and saves those who "lay deadly doing down" and cling to the cross, trusting the finished work of Christ ALONE for salvation. Have YOU come hat-in-hand to Calvary? Are you trusting the only Savior that God will ever provide for you? If you died today, would you spend eternity with Him, or be *forever* exiled from Him in a place our English Bibles call Hell?

The greatest mental anguish one could ever know is the eternal anguish of realizing that God loved us enough to buy Heaven for us, and that we could have had it as a free gift bought and paid for by God's Son upon Calvary's cross. But we spurned God's limitless love and rejected His infinite Grace. We said, "No!" to Heaven and

"Yes" to Hell. Whom will we blame forever, and ever, and ever, and ever, and ...?

I always hated homework until I started giving assignments to myself. Giving yourself "homework" can be fun. Give yourself this one assignment; it WILL change your life forever – it did mine. Start with Romans 1:1 and read through Hebrews 13:25. Have two highlighters of contrasting colors handy. Highlight every statement that refers to the lost (that's who you *were*!) in one color, and highlight everything that God says about the saved (that's who you *are*!) in the other color. You will be absolutely amazed at two things: how lost you were and how saved you are!

> "Roll back the curtain of memory now and then.
> Show me where you brought me from
> and where I could have been."
> – Dottie Rambo

Some churches never get you totally lost, and that's why they never get you totally saved. God only saves totally lost people! And He totally saves them! You can't come to Calvary partly lost, and you can't leave partly saved. If you are saved, your former position before the Judge of all the Earth was Hell-bound and Hell-deserving. Then God saw you united to fallen Adam, helpless and hopeless and deservedly so. Now He sees you in Christ His Son, dressed in gift righteousness, and having passed forever out of death and into life. Possessing "forever life."[14]

Remember, your standing is a work of God and, as such, can never be undone. It depends wholly on God's Grace.

Your state is your current degree of faithfulness to a loving Savior. How are you doing? Have you discovered that no one can live the Christian life? Have you discovered that Christ wants to live His life in and through you?

Does He?

CHAPTER EIGHT NOTES

1. Romans 5:6-9
2. Ephesians 1:22-23
3. Isaiah 64:6
4. Galatians 2:21
5. Hebrews 1:3
6. Revelation 21:5
7. Hebrews 1:10-12
8. II Corinthians 5:17
9. Romans 8:18-23
10. John 10:28-29
11. I Corinthians 15:53-54
12. Romans 6:12
13. Luke 19:10
14. John 5:24

CHAPTER NINE

GETTING IT STRAIGHT

God speaks! Faith, as defined in Scripture, is belief in what God has said.[1] In the Bible, God speaks to many individuals and groups. He speaks to fallen angels and men, to holy angels and men, to Jews and to Gentiles, to Christ, to Satan, to animals, and to inanimate creation. His message to different recipients differs greatly. What He says of Christ, "This is my beloved Son in whom I am well pleased,"[2] would not fit anyone but Christ; and certainly not Satan. His message to Satan would not fit anyone but Satan, and certainly not Christ. He told Noah to build a huge ark – but Noah only. You can't apply God's Word to Noah to your own case. If you do, you'd better build your ark outside; you'll never get it up the basement stairs!

All of the Bible is *for* us, but only part of the Bible is *to* us and *about* us!

God's directions to one group or individual may vary greatly from time to time also. He told unfallen Adam to stay in the Garden and be its landscaper. When Adam sinned, God told him to get out of the Garden and not to go back. For much of Peter's life he "kept kosher," then he was told "...eat...call not what I have cleansed common or unclean."[3] The Twelve were told not to carry wallets, then to carry them; not to go into the way of the Gentiles, then to go to the Gentiles, then to leave the Gentiles to Paul.[4] There is no contradiction if we "rightly divide," that is, if we distinguish God's will for a particular circumstance.

When the Twelve asked Christ, "Teach us to pray," He said, "When you pray, say, "Forgive us our trespasses as we forgive others their trespasses," then expounded that by saying, "For if you forgive not men their trespasses, neither will your Heavenly Father forgive your trespasses."[5] This was forgiveness under the Law – a system of command and penalty; a system of conditional blessing and cursing. To us, the Body of Christ, He says, "Forgive others, as God *has* forgiven you for Christ's sake."[6] This is forgiveness under Grace – a system of unconditional blessing.

God is not more limited in His use of language than we – He invented language. We use figures of speech and so does God.

Critics have mocked God and His Word because it speaks of sunrise and sunset, and we all know that the sun neither rises nor sets. But call Argonne National Laboratories and ask them what time the sun rises tomorrow and the scientists there will tell you. Don't those scientists know that the Earth turns but the Sun doesn't rise? Of course they do, but they are speaking figuratively – using the language of accommodation. Christ said, "Unless you eat the flesh of the Son of Man and drink His blood you have no life in you."[7] He explains that eating Him is a figure of speech meaning to come to Him, and that drinking of Him is a figure of speech signifying believing on Him. Scripture also says that "they [Israel in the Sinai] drank of that spiritual rock...and that Rock was Christ."[8] That can only mean that the rock was a type to be fulfilled in Christ, the Antitype, and that we would "drink" spiritually as they did physically.

He said, "I am the door," but He didn't mean that literally. He said, "I am the bread of life." Someone please tell that nameless, faceless monk in the dateless past that He didn't mean literal bread. The life being spiritual, the bread must also be spiritual. What a mess that unidentifiable monk made of a beautiful truth that God meant to be understood through the symbol. Christ called Herod a fox but He wasn't suggesting that Herod's parents hunted rabbits on all fours. I'm surprised that no medieval artist depicted Herod with a long, bushy tail.

Whole churches, each with millions of adherents, have taken as figurative God's promises of the nation Israel's future and applied those promises to themselves. Those promises made to Israel will be fulfilled to Israel and to no one else. God has staked His reputation on their literal fulfillment. It is our responsibility to distinguish what God means literally from what God means figuratively or God's meaning will be lost and our understanding will be unfruitful. We humans speak both literally and figuratively. So does God!

Don't pluck an eye out if it lusts for a girl in a miniskirt. You might run out of eyes! But don't miss the real meaning of the words. A figure always represents something literal. "...We have all been made to *drink* into one Spirit."[9] Ah ha!

Some of my dearest friends tell me that because men spoke in tongues in the Acts period, we must speak in tongues today because Christ cannot change. Men did not speak in tongues the day before Pentecost. Did Christ change when men "began" to speak in tongues? Christ doesn't change, but the Book of Acts is a book of constant changes. It is the Epistle to the Hebrews that tells us that "Christ is the same yesterday, today, and forever,"[10] but the Book of Hebrews is a book about monumental change.

God doesn't change, but He changes many things as His program advances.

I've visited many believers in mental health facilities who were there unnecessarily. Had they *studied* the Word as God has called all of us to do, and had they heeded it, perhaps they would not have wound up in a psych ward. A man I knew thirty years ago is facing death without one ounce of the peace that belongs to all believers. He made a deliberate decision to forego Bible study in favor of playing church and now has lost his assurance of salvation. He certainly did enjoy his little game of "church" and played it well, better than most, but had he studied his Savior in Scripture, he would be brimming with confidence now, and enjoying the anticipation of his homegoing. Instead, he is dreading the coming of the "death angel" and listening for his tread.

"Getting it straight" is another way of saying, "rightly dividing." We fail to rightly divide when we ignore the rule of *context*. A radio preacher that I occasionally hear believes that God does not love the world of men, that Christ did not die for all, and that not everyone who hears can believe and be saved. He constantly quotes John 6:44, "No man can come to me except the Father draw him." Like many who share his Augustinianism, he never quotes John 6:45, the very next verse, where Christ explains *how* the Father draws men to the Son. "As it is written, 'They shall all be taught by the Father.' Everyone therefore that has heard from the Father and has learned, comes to me." "Faith [always] comes by the thing heard, and the thing heard from the Word."[11]

If God hasn't said it, you can't believe it! If God *has* said it, *ANYONE* hearing it can believe it and be saved. Has the Father drawn you to the Son? Does He continue to draw you to Him?

God is not Lewis Carroll, and He did not write "Jabberwocky." God wrote His Word to be understood. "The entrance to thy Word gives off light. It gives understanding to the simple."[12] No man, even in a lifetime of study, can understand everything in the Bible – it is a boundless and fathomless flood. As a matter of fact, God calls it "a great deep" or "mighty ocean."[13] I believe that we shall be studying who and what God is for all eternity. God is inexhaustible. How could finite beings, even glorified finite beings, know everything there is to know about the infinite God? One would have to be God to know God perfectly. But then, I don't know everything about ingesting, digesting, and metabolizing food, but I keep right on with the ingesting part. I use my knife and fork like there's no tomorrow.

Learn to use your "knife and fork" on the written bread of life. All of the Bible is for us; the message of Christ risen and glorified (the Pauline Epistles) is *to* us and *about* us. Study the *whole* Bible; *major* in the Pauline Epistles. There were twelve circumcision Apostles. They are to sit on twelve thrones judging the twelve tribes of Israel.[14] When Judas defected and lost his Apostleship – and with it his future throne, he had to be replaced. Eleven Apostles would be one too few to govern twelve tribes. Thirteen would be one too many. Paul is not one of the Twelve, nor the thirteenth. He did not keep company with Christ and the others from the baptism of John to the ascension of Christ.[15] That disqualifies him from being one of the Twelve. Paul is "that other and different Apostle." He distinguishes himself from the Twelve and they recognize the distinction.[16]

They are circumcision Apostles. He is *the* Apostle to the Gentiles – the Apostle of the uncircumcision.[17] Their ministry was set aside in the Acts period because Israel refused God and Peter's offer of the Kingdom. You can't offer a King to France, Kenya, Thailand, or Chile when that King has to have a throne in, and rule over, Israel. This is why twelve men commissioned "to go...into all the world" never went. The thirty plus years covered by the Book of Acts record no worldwide ministry of the Twelve. Paul goes to hundreds of thousands of Gentiles; Peter goes to one – Cornelius.

Paul never considers himself better than the Twelve. As a matter of fact, he says that he himself is not fit to be an Apostle because he persecuted believers until he met the Lord.[18] But he also says that he had more "revelations," (personal appearances of Christ), than all of them put together. And that he labored more than they all.[19] This is not bragging – it is teaching dispensationally, rightly dividing, "getting it straight." Their program was being set aside. They could not offer a king to Somalia, Tibet, or The United States until He was accepted in Jerusalem.

Fifteen centuries earlier, God made the choice of Moses to play a role in Israel that He gave to no one else to play. Moses' brother Aaron and sister Miriam objected. They wanted God to share the leadership of Israel and give them a piece of the action. The experts, two hundred and fifty rulers, wanted a share too. A couple of million Israelis also balked at the singular nature of Moses' "Apostleship." So Moses' relatives, the "experts" in the nation, and the consensus agreed against God's choice of Moses.

A similar thing has taken place with God's selection of Paul to be uniquely the Apostle for the Body of Christ. Today's experts – church leaders, denominational heads, seminary professors, evangelists, pastors, and teachers alike – resist the Scriptures' plain teaching on the unique Apostleship and distinctive message of the Apostle Paul. If you point out that what is called "church truth," while it is alluded to, is never introduced or developed by non-Pauline authors, they say you make too much of Paul. If you explain that in Scripture, the Twelve learn the Grace Message from Paul, they say you make too much of Paul. If you demonstrate that only eight books of the New Testament are written by the Twelve (only three of them wrote

Scripture), and that their books are evidently addressed to Jews and about things Jewish, they again complain that you make too much of Paul. It is certainly a sin to be a *Paulist* – to make too much of Paul; it is also a great sin to refuse to be *Pauline* – to follow Paul as he follows Christ.[20]

Speaking of *himself,* Paul humbly confesses, "I am nothing;" "I am the least of the apostles;" "I am less than the least of ALL saints."[21] But speaking of his special God-given *ministry* he says, "I [singularly] am the Apostle of the Gentiles;" "I am not a whit behind the chiefest [Apostles];" and "[I] worked harder than 'all';" "Unto me [singularly] was committed a dispensation,"[22] etc.

Christ spoke in the prophets, say God and Peter.[23] Christ spoke in His earthly ministry, and what God felt we should have of what He said is recorded by Matthew, Mark, Luke and John. Christ spoke again from Heaven, and most of this message is to the "Body Church" through Paul.

Shall we be like Miriam, Aaron, the two hundred and fifty rulers of Israel and the Israeli multitudes who hardened their hearts in unbelief and rebelled against God by rebelling against Moses?[24] Or shall we accept God's choice of His "chosen vessel"[25] for the Body of Christ?

Let's plug our spiritual umbilical cords into the Word of God. Will this make us fanatics? Were the martyrs fanatics? When an early Christian denied Christ as the result of torture, a "secret believer," a sixteen year old girl stepped forward to take his place. She died from the torture. She died for Christ.[26] Was she a fanatic? The truth is that *all* of us should be zealots. We cannot serve two masters. We will love one and hate the other. We serve Christ or we serve sin – zealously. "He that is not with me is against me."[27]

"O Earth, Earth, Earth, hear the Word of the Lord."[28] Man's chief responsibility is the regular intake of Bible doctrine. For us who have been saved, the responsibility to acquaint ourselves with the Word of God so that we might do the will of God intensifies. I am responsible to get all the light that I can, but more light brings with it more responsibility.

"Your words were found and I did eat them, and your Word was to me the joy and rejoicing of my heart."[29]

When God's Word ceases to be the great adventure and excitement of my life, when Christ ceases to be my happiness, I am sick, seriously ill, dangerously ill. And only the Word can make me well again.

CHAPTER NINE NOTES

1. Romans 10:17
2. Matthew 3:17
3. Acts 10:9-17
4. Matthew 10:5-10 with Galatians 2:7-9
5. Matthew 6:14-15
6. Ephesians 4:32
7. John 6:53
8. I Corinthians 10:4
9. I Corinthians 12:13
10. Hebrews 13:8
11. Romans 10:17
12. Psalm 119:130
13. Psalm 36:6
14. Matthew 19:27-28
15. Acts 1:21-26
16. Galatians 2:6-9
17. Romans 11:13
18. I Corinthians 15:9
19. I Corinthians 15:10-11; II Corinthians 11:23
20. I Corinthians 11:1; 4:16; I Thessalonians 1:6
21. I Corinthians 3:6-7; 15:9; II Corinthians 12:11; Ephesians 3:8
22. Romans 11:13; II Corinthians 11:5; Ephesians 3:2
23. I Peter 1:10-11
24. Numbers 12:1-9; Numbers 16: 1-2, 35, 49
25. Acts 9:15
26. Foxe's Book of Martyrs
27. Matthew 12:30
28. Jeremiah 22:29
29. Jeremiah 15:16

CHAPTER TEN

TWO PROGRAMS

I was instantly, completely, and eternally saved when I was 20 years old, but no matter how much I read the Bible, I didn't understand much of it until I was forty. I had twenty long years of knowing Christ as Savior, but not understanding fundamental truths about salvation, life and ministry – truths we need to know and to grasp to live according to God's will in Satan's world.

Millions of people in this world today have been born twice: born of Adam – born from below, and then born of God – born from above. And for these millions of born again Christians, new birth brought with it a new desire: a desire "...to will and to do of His good pleasure,"[1] but most do not have a clue as to what God has done for them in the past, what He is busy doing for them today, nor what He will accomplish in the future.

A light went on when I first realized that the great key that unlocks the Scriptures is *"the Gospel of the Grace of Christ"*[2] – the good news of the *Mystery*. This one key opens many doors, solves many mysteries, and answers many questions. Take the mystery of "the Church which is His Body."[3] God tells us that there are three classes of people in today's world: Jews, Gentiles, and the Assembly (lit. "the outcalled") of God.[4] This "outcalling" is the "one new man" of Ephesians 2:15. One new man made of two old ones, God having – in Christ – taken down the middle wall of partition between Jew and Gentile by abolishing the Law that divided and stood between us.[5]

A simple, though little known, key to Bible understanding is this: *there are two major programs in Scripture and in history.* "In the beginning God created the Heavens and the Earth."[6] He had already planned a Heavenly Kingdom program for a heavenly people and an Earthly Kingdom program for an earthly people. Twelve-thirteenths of the Bible concern the Earthly program and one-thirteenth the Heavenly program. God never confuses these two programs, nor should we. To confuse these two programs, as religion consistently does, is to twist the Scriptures to our own ruin.[7]

If you and I seek to apply verses to man under Grace that can only apply to man under Law, we will be making sense into nonsense. There are many truths that transcend dispensational boundaries, and there are many that do not. If we are to understand God and His Word, we must recognize the distinctions that God makes in Scripture. The Body of Christ is neither "Spiritual Israel" nor "The Israel of God." God *HAS NOT* replaced Israel with the Church! God has staked His reputation on the future fulfillment of His many promises made to His favored nation. Israel's darkest night and most glorious sunrise are still ahead – maybe *just* ahead! The Church is not Israel extended, warmed over, or replaced. We have our destiny and Israel has hers. When we read a promise in Scripture, we must make sure that it's addressed to us!

All of the Bible is *FOR* us and we should study it daily. The Pauline Epistles are to us and about us and we should major in them. God chose Moses to play a unique role in Israel, and Israel did not like God's choice. God chose Paul to play a unique role in the Body of Christ, and the Body of Christ does not like it. Tough toenails! God isn't going to budge on Moses or Paul! God knows what He's doing, Friend. He doesn't need advice from you and me. He decided, in eternity past to communicate ALL "church truth" through Paul's 14 Epistles. Peter, John, James, and Jude may reflect "Grace truth," even allude to it, but they never introduce it nor develop it! That province God gave to one Apostle. In Galatians two, the Twelve agreed to confine their ministry to Israel while turning world evangelism over to "that new and different Apostle." Like Israel, we can hate it or love it. I love it! It is the will of God and Christ!

God promised that the same people that He scattered in judgment He will regather in blessing.[8] God scattered the nation of Israel in judgment, not the Presbyterian, Catholic, or Lutheran Church. Not the Mormons or the Jehovah's Witnesses. ISRAEL! It would be uproariously funny if it weren't tragically sad to read the paragraph headings in some Bibles that say, "Judgments on Israel" over one paragraph, and then "Blessings on the Church" over the next. How did the Church, any Church, get into God's prophetic view of Israel's future? God didn't author those paragraph headings, wishful thinkers with their own agenda did! To leave Israel with all of her promised judgments while robbing her of all her promised future blessings is dishonest and evil.

The Body of Christ has abundant blessings of our own; we don't have to rob God's favored nation of the future glory promised her in the day that she returns to God and to her destiny as "the head of the nations and not the tail."[9]

It is not only future but also past promises to Jews that are stolen by some Christians. "I am the Lord, who gives you the power to get wealth."[10a] To whom was this promise made? "I am the Lord who heals you."[10b] To whom was this promise given? Paul, the steward of the Dispensation of Grace, was frequently hungry, thirsty, and cold, and without adequate funds.[11] Did he not know of the "prosperity gospel"? He was ill and was given grace instead of healing.[12] Timothy was frequently ill.[13] Trophimus was so sick that he had to be dropped from Paul's team on an important Apostolic tour.[14] Epaphroditus was seriously ill for months, and almost died on Paul's hands.[15] Where was "faith healing" in these instances?

It's been noted that, "You can prove anything by a verse from the Bible," but does the whole Bible support your claim or doctrine? A man in a western suburb of Chicago read in Genesis that Adam and Eve were naked and unashamed. Had he read further, he would have learned that, after the Fall, God Himself clothed them. Had he read the Gospels, he could have learned that we "have need" of clothing. Had he read Peter, he might have learned that clothing is meant to provide needed modesty, but he didn't read further. He didn't do his homework. He stripped and streaked. He became locally famous for dashing up and down supermarket aisles "in the buff." His troubles with the local constabulary arose because he took one verse and stopped. He chose willful ignorance over the wisdom that comes from "rightly dividing the Word of Truth."

God wrote the Bible to be understood. No one person could possibly understand all of it, but *everyone must* understand what it says about salvation, and every believer *must* understand what it says about how we should live and minister.

God tells the Romans (and us!), that we are to present ourselves to Him as alive from the dead, because WE ROSE WHEN CHRIST ROSE. Nearly all Christians come before God in prayer, not as "alive from the dead," not as already in possession of resurrection life, with all of its privileges and powers, but as beggars on probation. God tells us that while sin is very much alive in us, we have died to sin legally, positionally, and actually, and sin is no longer the issue. Now the issue is faith – believing God and walking with Him in our new and permanent standing as risen with Christ.[16]

How many Christians believe that the standing they had when in union with Adam no longer exists – nor can it? That it has been permanently and eternally replaced by a new standing with God that can never be lessened or lost because it is based on who Christ is and what Christ has done, and not dependent on them at all? How many Christians do *you* know who truly believe that the person they were in Adam no longer exists? That their old man died and their present life is hidden with Christ in God? How many live as though they believe this? How many preachers can you name who preach this as if they really believe it? How many preachers even know that this is clearly taught in that body of Scripture that sets forth God's new, and hitherto kept hidden, program? You won't have to take your shoes off to count them. Are you surprised at this? Did not God predict that church history would be characterized by a rejection of God's truth and an eager embrace of falsehood by both pulpit and pew?

"For the time will come when they will not tolerate sound teaching; but after their own lusts shall heap to themselves teachers, having itching ears; and they shall turn away their ears from the truth, and shall be turned unto fables."[17] Did you spot your favorite

Mega-church in here? That this time began in the very first century of church history is evident by the fact that Paul tells Timothy how to deal with it. Nor is there any hint in Scripture that the Church would ever recover from its fall. Eutychus fell asleep while Paul was "long preaching," and did not awaken until Paul was used by God to awaken him.[18] The Church fell down from its lofty height early in Paul's long (already 1900 year) ministry, and won't awaken until and unless it is awakened by God through Paul. Francis L. Patton, onetime President of Princeton, said, "The only hope of Christianity is in the rehabilitation of the Pauline theology. It is back, back, back to an incarnate Christ and the atoning blood, or it is on, on, on to atheism and despair."

The Heavenly Kingdom program – our program – ends, as a distinct dispensation with the recall of Christ's ambassadors from Planet Earth before the outbreak of hostilities that will usher in the initial stage of the Day of the Lord. This recall is accomplished through the miracle of the Rapture, when "The dead in Christ shall rise and we the living who remain shall be caught up together with them to meet the Lord in the air."[19] When Christ left Earth at the end of His first advent, He ascended to Heaven in a glorified human body, without benefit of a space shuttle. Slowly to the clouds, then instantly to Heaven's throne.[20]

I was a guest speaker in a *Bible as Literature* class in an Elgin, Illinois high school. Near the end of my lecture, a student in the back row raised her hand to ask, "What about the Rapture?" The teacher lost it. She exploded in an uncontrolled burst of hilarious laughter. "Oh," she giggled, "the Rapture. That's when millions of people leave the Earth without a rocket and fly to Heaven." Turning to the teacher, I asked, "Where is Christ right now?" No answer. "Doesn't the Word of God teach that He was translated, or 'Raptured'? Caught up to Heaven? And did He bother with rockets?" I didn't intend to embarrass the teacher, but I couldn't let her ridicule of Scripture go unanswered.

Christ's first advent included many miracles – supernatural events, things that can't be explained by natural means and were not part of the "normal" course of events. Christ's very coming to Earth as the God-Man was in itself miraculous, as was His departure before eye witnesses. His return to the atmosphere to catch away His heavenly people before returning to Earth itself to rescue and reign over His earthly people, and through them over the entire globe will be a divine intervention made possible only by the setting aside of laws with which we have become familiar.

After a Bible class one day, a woman came to the platform to thank us for the teaching. "You made one statement today," she said, "that answered a thousand questions for me." What could I possibly say in a single statement that could answer that many questions? "Well," said the lady, "you said that when God concludes the present Dispensation of Grace with the miracle of the Rapture, He will then reach down and restart his prophetic clock and begin to deal with the world once more through His favored nation, Israel. I had a long list of questions to ask you, but that statement is the key to answering them all."

The coming Millennium will surely be ablaze with the glory of God, especially following on the heels of the Great Tribulation (history's greatest nightmare by far). Satan and his sub-alterns will be imprisoned for the entire one thousand years. War, poverty, sickness, and death (except for rare applications of capital punishment) will be banished too. The Earth will produce so bountifully that people will have to clean out their pantries regularly to make room for new and fresh supplies. Man, having more than enough for the first time since the Fall, will glorify God. Christ will reign over a peaceful Earth and righteous peoples. "The knowledge of God will cover the Earth as the waters cover the sea."[21] Adventures will be safe, enterprises profitable, and relationships rewarding. Even the animal kingdom will exist in harmony.

Yet all of this is not to be compared with the unequaled privilege that belongs to the Body of Christ in this Dispensation of Grace. True, our lives are fraught with difficulty and threatened by dangers. Incredible suffering can, in a moment, become our lot. Defeat, disappointment, discouragement, and depression surround us. Broken dreams, broken hearts, and broken lives strew our pathways, and sometimes the pain of brokenness is *ours*. Alexander MacLaren said, "Be kind, nearly everyone you meet in life is fighting a battle!"

But Christ dwells within and we have the privileged adventure of worshiping and serving Him in Satan's world, in an evil age, in a hostile environment, in a difficult time, surrounded by problems and indwelt by fears. We will worship and serve Him forever in eternity future, but never, ever, will we be able to "present [our] bodies living sacrifices"[22] in the face of this present challenge. Never will the gift of our lives to our Savior mean more to Him than it does this minute.

The road is sometimes rough, the battles frightening, and the war costly, but it is more than worth it all because we do it for our Lord, who gave all – even Himself to a cross – for us!

In future ages, five star generals in the angelic community will stand at the curb and salute us as we pass, not because of who we are, nor even because of what we may have done, but because of who Christ is and how He has graced us!

> "Only one life,'twill soon be past.
> Only what's done for Christ will last."

Are you living your one brief life for Him?

CHAPTER TEN NOTES

1. Philippians 2:13
2. Galatians 1:6
3. Ephesians 1:22-23
4. I Corinthians 10:32
5. Ephesians 2:14-18
6. Genesis 1:1
7. II Peter 3:16
8. Deuteronomy 4:27 with Deuteronomy 30:3-6
9. Deuteronomy 28:13
10. a. Deuteronomy 8:18; b. Exodus 15:26
11. II Corinthians 11:22-27; Philippians 4:10-16
12. II Corinthians 12:6-10
13. I Timothy 5:23
14. II Timothy 4:20
15. Philippians 2:25-30
16. Romans 6:1-4
17. II Timothy 4:3-4
18. Acts 20:7-12
19. I Thessalonians 4:13-18
20. Acts 1:9-11
21. Isaiah 11:9
22. Romans 12:1

CHAPTER ELEVEN

TWO GOSPELS

~

"There's only one gospel, brother!" I've heard it a hundred times. True, there is only one gospel to be preached today. Only one that God can bless. Only one that can save us sinners from eternal ruin, but there have been other gospels.

Gospel is an old word meaning "good news." Scripture didn't invent it; it was in common use in the Greek-speaking world of the first century. While it always means "good news," *which* good news must be determined by context.

The "good news" that Abraham received and believed was, "In you shall all the Gentiles be blessed."[1] That was good news, sure enough, but it was not the good news that you and I believe to be saved, that "Christ died for our sins."[2] Timothy brought good news (lit. translation of "gospel") of the faith and love of the Thessalonians to Paul.[3] Again, while this was certainly good news – or gospel – it was not the good news that produces saving faith in sinners who receive it.

The Twelve, commissioned "to preach the kingdom of God, and to heal the sick," went through the towns "preaching the gospel, and healing everywhere."[4] What gospel did they preach as they performed miraculous signs? The good news of the coming Earthly Kingdom of Christ. It could not possibly have been the good news of Christ's coming death for sinners, for at least two years later when Christ began to tell them that He was about to die, "They understood *none* of these things, and this saying was *hidden* from them, *neither knew they* the things that were spoken." Luke 18:34 tells us in three different ways that these twelve men, who had been preaching a divinely originated gospel for at least two years, (1) understood nothing of Christ's impending death, (2) the truth of His death had been hidden from them, and (3) they still didn't get it when He told them.

When the Holy Spirit speaks periphrastically, using more words than are strictly necessary to make a point, we recognize two things: the super importance of what is being emphasized, and the fact that God is patient with us in our capacity to be obtuse, or "blockheaded." God has had to tell me some things many times before they sank into my concrete head, and even then the Holy Spirit has had to remind me of wonderful truths that I know but seem prone to forget – to shelve in some dark store-room of my mind.

The book of Galatians – the study of which is so sorely needed by today's church and so seldom taught – condemns the proclaiming of any other gospel than "Paul's Gospel."[5] We may, and we should, teach *about* the gospel of the Kingdom, but we are to proclaim and to offer to a lost world only the good news of Christ's death on behalf of lost sinners. And we are forbidden to offer Christ to the world as Israel's Messiah, the Man of Galilee, the Lowly Nazarene, and proclaim Kingdom truth as though it were the saving good news for today. Believing that Christ is Israel's Messiah is a good thing, but believing this will save neither Jew nor Gentile today.

The saving message today is the good news of Christ's Grace in dying man's death, and no other message is "the power of God unto salvation"![6] Mixing these two gospels – the good news of the future Millennial reign of the Son of Man, and the good news of the death, burial, and resurrection of the Son of God – always brings confusion and frequently abject ruin to people today.

The Gospel of the Kingdom, or Millennial reign of Christ, was and – updated by the cross and empty tomb – will be again preached to Israel and through Israel to the Gentile world. It was never intended to be preached by the Body of Christ. The Body of Christ began after Israel rejected God the Father and His testimony in the period of the prophets, God the Son and His testimony in the period of the Gospels, and God the Spirit and His testimony in early Acts. When, in early Acts, Israel refused God and Peter's offer of the return of Christ to reign, they committed the unpardonable sin. This sin could ONLY be committed in the first century and by the nation of Israel. No one has committed the unpardonable sin since, AND NO ONE CAN!

When you hear a Bible teacher mixing the good news of the Millennium with the good news of Christ's Grace, don't be judgmental, unkind, and arrogant. Love him and pray for him. Be a loving Christian. "Be kind," said MacLaren, "Nearly everyone you meet in life is fighting a battle." And don't forget what Will Rogers said: "Be humble, we're all ignorant, we're just ignorant about different things." God says to you and to me, "Be kind."[7] So-o-o-o-o-o, be kind! And pray for me that I'll be kind too! However, if your church is adamantly dedicated to preaching a wrong gospel, thank your pastor sincerely for what he has done for you, and move on – quietly. Don't impeach the pastor, don't split the church, don't start the First Church of Spite across the street, and don't try to take the congregation with you. Just move on. Somewhere there's a church where you can grow – that's what churches are for, even if you must "attend" by listening to the teaching on the internet, the radio, a CD, or a tape, etc. Moving on is better than causing trouble. It is not our calling to set every one straight. Sometimes God is honored by our leaving some people to Heaven and going on with our own maturing and ministering. I wouldn't call anyone to tell them why I left. If someone called me to ask, I'd tell them honestly and graciously. But, remember, God is not looking for people to split churches. That's more the Devil's stock in trade and he always has more help than he needs.

"Every Scripture is God-breathed and profitable...."[8] You and I cannot emphasize that enough. "Every Scripture" means the whole Word, from Genesis 1:1 to Revelation 22:21. Our Lord said, "Man shall live...by every word that proceeds from the mouth of God."[9] The entire Bible is *FOR* us and we should study the entire Bible. The message of Christ risen and glorified addressed to the Body of Christ, (a.k.a. the Pauline Epistles), is *TO* us and *ABOUT* us! The whole Bible is our field of study. Our major must be the Epistles of the risen Christ – Romans through Hebrews. No matter how many times I say this, and I've said it literally thousands of times, someone, even some Christian leader, will tell the world that I limit Christians to the Pauline Epistles. The WHOLE Bible is for us!

> "There was a little girl who had a little curl
> right in the middle of her forehead.
> And when she was good, she was very, very good
> and when she was bad, she was horrid!"
> – Henry Wadsworth Longfellow

All Bible teachers are good when they're good and bad when they're bad. All believers are good when they're good, and bad when they're bad. The worst of us are right when we're right and the best of us are wrong when we're wrong. You and I included! Ask yourself, " Is the Bible REALLY my sole rule of faith and practice? The Bible rightly divided? Or is my faith partly groupthink?" Groupthink! Satan's gift that keeps on giving.

When I asked a foreign missionary, "What is your hope of Heaven? What are the grounds of your assurance of salvation?" He replied, "I've put my hand to the plow handle, and I'm not looking back." I kid you not! His "assurance" came from a discipleship verse, not a salvation verse. It was addressed by Christ, when under Law, to Jews under Law anticipating entering the Millennial Kingdom. This man was associated with a world famous para-church ministry, and his hope of Heaven was something he himself had done and was doing. That's enough to make a buzzard barf – or should be!

Christ died a complete death for completely lost and ruined sinners. He is a complete Savior and He always and only saves completely! When sinners, or even saints, add something to the crosswork of our Lord they take everything away from it. It doesn't matter if the "thing" added is a Protestant thing, a Catholic thing, an Orthodox thing, or an Evangelical thing. Sinners are saved when they bring their sins to Calvary – not their "things," not their virtues or their works.[10] Leave your "things" behind, and don't go back after them. That was *YOUR* death that *HE* died; He had no death of His own to die. Death had no claim on Him. He came voluntarily into the realm of death for you, and when He died your death, He bore the wrath of God for YOU. He paid the debt you couldn't pay, paid it in full, and God never collects a debt twice!

The person you WERE, in sin and under condemnation, died with Him. You were buried with Him, and raised with Him. You are now to present yourself to Him "as alive from the dead," because you ARE alive from the dead! Just as much alive as Christ Himself![11] Whenever you are conscious of having sinned, thank God that all your sins, past, present and future – yesterday's and tomorrow's – have been forgiven and then depend on the power of Christ within to enable you to forsake that sin. The fact that tomorrow's sins are already forgiven is the greatest impetus to holiness that the world will ever see! If knowing that God has not only erased your blackboard, but thrown your blackboard away does not make you want to know Him better, love Him more, and worship and serve Him always, *nothing* will. Grace works! It was Paul's motivation for serving Christ in spite of floggings, beatings, hunger, thirst, inadequate shelter, shipwrecks, imprisonments, being forsaken by friends, deserted by co-workers, and hunted by enemies. Grace worked for Paul and it will work for you. *Is* it working for you? Are you living the Grace-driven life? Do you want to?

You and I are living in what one expositor called "The Great Parenthesis," and another has labeled "The Divine Interregnum." Scripture calls it the Dispensation, or Stewardship of Grace.[12] Israel having refused God and Peter's offer of the return of Christ to reign, refusing to become the prophesied kingdom of priests to the Gentile world, God has temporarily abandoned the Earthly Kingdom program and inserted a new and unprophesied program not centered in the nation Israel. The Heavenly program has at its core the Body of Christ. The Earthly program had an incomplete revelation, saw "as in a [mirror] obscurely," and needed evidential signs and revelatory gifts.[13] Its Twelve Apostles virtually disappear one third of the way through the Book of Acts and a new and different Apostle comes center stage. Those who were to go into all the world DID NOT, even agreeing with the new Apostle to confine their ministry to Israel and leave Gentile ministry to him.[14] In early Acts one of the Twelve – Peter – goes to one Gentile – Cornelius – and the rest of Acts is a recital concerning the divine setting aside of Israel and another Apostle's ministry to hundreds of thousands of Gentiles. That God was turning from the nation Israel to the Gentiles in Acts is a self-evident truth.[15] That God will return to Israel when Israel returns to God is repeatedly promised in both Testaments.

Israel's program – with its wonders, powers, and signs and with its miraculous gifts, with its incomplete information requiring the word of knowledge, word of wisdom, tongues, interpretations, discerning of spirits, circumcision, holy days, feasts, Sabbaths, sprinklings, splashings, dunkings, and walking by sight (lit. "appearance") – has given way to our program with its completed canon of Scripture and its walk by faith (in God's Word). Some similarities, but many differences!

Israel lived under a system of conditional blessing called Law; we live under a system of unconditional blessing called Grace. Israel's program was just what the doctor ordered for Israel. Our program is perfect for us. We have no need of those blessings which were peculiar to Israel; and they had no possibility of procuring the blessings that are uniquely ours.[16] Some Christians wrongly assume that, "every promise in the book is mine." They miss the many superior blessings that are ours by confusing the two major economies and placing themselves under the conditions and limitations imposed on Israel, some of which will be lifted when Israel returns to God, accepts Christ, and enters into her promised glory.

There will be no sickness when the King is reigning on Earth. It would be amusing if it were not tragic, to see some preachers today wearing glasses to read healing verses and laying hands on the sick while suffering themselves from crippling arthritis. When today's health, wealth, and happiness crowd unleashes their miraculous power in Children's Hospital, and empties the wards, they'll get my attention. Until then, it's hard to take their medicine show seriously. Many of their followers are dear people with irresistible personalities, individual graces, and good intentions, but bad doctrine – due to a lack of sound Bible teaching from the Word of Truth rightly divided. They just keep trying to continue a dispensation that God has packed in ice until His present administration has run its course and concluded with the miracle of the translation, or "Rapture."

Meet you in the clouds!

CHAPTER ELEVEN NOTES

1. Galatians 4:8; Genesis 12:3; 18:18; 22:18; 26:4; 28:14
2. I Corinthians 15:3
3. I Thessalonians 3:6
4. Luke 9:1-6
5. Galatians 1:6-9
6. I Corinthians 1:8
7. Ephesians 4:32
8. II Timothy 3:16-17
9. Matthew 4:4
10. Titus 3:5
11. Romans 6:9-14
12. Ephesians 3:1-9
13. I Corinthians 13:8-13
14. Galatians 2:6-9
15. Acts 13:46; 18:6; 28:25-28
16. Romans 16:25-26

CHAPTER TWELVE

TWO INVITATIONS

The Philippian jailor asked his prisoner, "What must I do to be saved?" The prisoner, our Apostle Paul, replied simply, "Believe on the Lord Jesus Christ and you will be saved."[1] The jailor was to "do" only one thing – the only thing that he could "do" without doing anything! God had shut him up to faith. To be saved, he needed only to believe, because believing is the only thing we can "do" to be saved. God does not accept anything less than total trust in the Savior that He has provided. God saves us by Grace through trust and anything other than trust would be less than trust. Nor does God accept anything *more* than trust. Anything *more* than trust would be *other* than trust too. We cannot add man's merit to God's Grace and still have God's Grace, any more than we can add arsenic to nursery water and still have nursery water.[2]

To repent means to re-think, to change one's mind. "Repent and believe the Gospel" simply means, "change your mind and believe the Gospel." One moment you don't believe that Christ died *YOUR* death; the next moment you do. You "repented." You changed your mind from not believing to believing – from unbelief to faith. It was one operation, not two. It was not "feel sorry for your sins and believe;" that would be two things, one a work and the other faith. It was not "change your life and believe;" that would involve many works in addition to faith, but God saves by Grace through faith, plus nothing![3] Anything additional to faith, or trust, would be works, and your works were not only ignored but rejected at Calvary.

The Philippian jailor was to do the believing and God would do the saving. The result is guaranteed. Paul did not say, "Believe and you *might* be saved," but "Believe...and you *will* be saved." Not one single sinner ever believed God concerning the death of His son and failed to be saved. If we do all the believing, God will ALWAYS do all the saving. Some teach that we are to do the best that we can and God will make up the deficit through Calvary. Others teach that God does some, or even most, of the saving through Calvary and that then we must provide the rest. Either way, we become our own Savior. Both of these views are argued on the false premise that God is a Maxwell Street merchant making deals with men. They imply that God would be foolish to save people who do nothing to earn, merit, or deserve their salvation. But man can do nothing to satisfy the just demands of God's infinite holiness. An eternity spent working for God would not remove one little sin. Nor would an eternity in a "purgatory" remove the least of our sins.

Only Calvary removes sin! Only Calvary *can* remove sin![4] And Calvary removes ALL sin! Thank God, because you and I cannot enter Heaven with even one sin charged to our account. Eating one bite of forbidden fruit cost not only Adam the individual, but Adam the race the whole ball game. One sin – the sin of the race committed in Adam's garden when we ALL sinned – plunged all of humanity into complete and awful ruin for eternity![5] Using the language of accommodation, we might say, "God searched the Universe for a way to rectify man's ruin and not just the best way, but the only way He could find was sending His Son to a cruel and criminal cross to be our Substitute, to bear the just wrath of God for us, to pay our debt in full." You may say that you don't understand it. No one does! You don't have to, anymore than you have to understand how "a black cow eats green grass that turns into white milk and is churned into yellow butter and puts red hair on a freckle-faced boy."[6] The Philippian jailor didn't understand it either, not even the Apostle Paul, but Paul believed it and preached it. The jailor believed it too, and he was instantly, completely, and eternally saved.

She was a beautiful young woman indeed and the judges crowned her "Miss America." She said she was dedicated to helping the world to find peace, and said that she couldn't have won the crown if she hadn't "asked Jesus into [her] heart." She was a dear person who loved God, and Christ, and the Bible, and Christians. She displayed what seemed a sincere compassion for others, but the salvation message is not "ask Jesus into your heart;" it is "believe on the Lord Jesus Christ and you will be saved." It is not "commit your life to God," "give your heart to Jesus," or anything like that. You and I, and Miss America, came empty-handed to the cross where we did only the believing and God made good on His promise to save.

If God could remain just while accepting anything you are or anything you do, Christ died for nothing.[7] If Christ's death provided 99% of your salvation, you would still be 100% lost until you anteed up your one percent, and when you did you would be your own Savior.

God did not say, "Do the best you can, and Christ's death will make up the deficit;" He would be treating the "filthy rags"[8] of human righteousness on a par with His own infinitely pure righteousness, and fallen man's works on a par with His Son's crosswork. Man always wants to "do" something to be saved. If you or I could "do" anything, the death of God's sinless Son would be without purpose. That would make Christ foolish for going to the cross, and His Father a monster for sending Him there.

Religion is all about *"doing,"* and salvation is all about *"done."* God's Son says from Calvary's cross, "Finished, completed, paid in full."[9] When man attempts to "do" something to be saved, man is saying, "unfinished, incomplete, paid in part."

What do you say?

> "Do this and live," the Law commands,
> but gives me neither feet nor hands.
> A better word the Gospel brings;
> it bids me fly, and gives me wings."

The Philippian jailor, like all of us, wanted to do something to receive salvation. It is an easy thing for religion to make a person think, "I am *hell-bound*." But the man who gives up trying to "do" something for God, and simply comes empty-handed to an ugly, blood-stained, urine-soaked, feces-encrusted cross, and accepts as a free gift the salvation offered there, is believing "I am *hell-deserving*." God has never saved "a diamond in the rough." He only saves "garbage for the dump" – people who are headed for Gehenna – and deserve to be!

Don't insult your Creator by trying to come to the cross as a Superbowl quarterback, or a beauty-pageant queen. Don't come in a tux or an evening gown. Ladies and Gentlemen don't have a Savior. Only sinners have a Savior! And don't accept a counterfeit savior. The only real Savior is crucified, risen, and coming again.

"Jesus said to him, 'I am the Way, the Truth, and the Life: No man comes to the Father, but by *ME*!"[10]

Next time you hear an evangelist, pastor, Bible teacher, or a Christian who is witnessing say, "There are seven things you must do to be saved," (or four, or three, or even two), remember the words of God and Paul, "Believe on the Lord Jesus Christ, and you will be saved."[11]

There are two invitations being given today. Religion's invitation says, "Do this and you might be saved." God's invitation says, "It's all been done; 'Believe on the Lord Jesus Christ and you will be saved.'" A gift is always something totally free to one party because it is fully paid for by another! Anything less than that might be a bargain, but it wouldn't be a gift. God is very clear on the matter of our salvation. "The wages of sin is death, but the free gift of God is eternal life in Christ Jesus our Lord."[12] A wage is what we have earned. A gift, by its very nature, cannot be earned. To tell someone that salvation is a gift, and then tell him how to earn it is nonsense. You cannot work for a gift; what you work for is wages. To tell someone that Grace is unmerited favor – and it is! – and then tell him what he must do to merit it is foolishness. To say that Grace is undeserved kindness – and it is! – and then tell people how to deserve it is a monstrously bad joke.

We all start life ignorant. The Bible tells us that the fear of the Lord is the beginning of knowledge...and wisdom.[13] Before we can become wise, we must acknowledge that, without Christ, we are fools.[14] The cross – where God paid an incredibly high price for our salvation – an infinitely higher price than will ever be paid for anything or anyone in all of eternity, is foolishness to the once-born man. But the cross is "the wisdom of God."[15] You and I don't really understand it – no one does – but God believes it and teaches it in His Word. The cross, so repugnant to fallen man's "intellect," is actually the genius of God. One day this will be clear to angels and men. All angels and all men! "Now is the accepted time, now is the day of salvation."[16] When the day of salvation concludes, there will be no more offer of salvation for deservedly lost human beings. When the day of salvation is over, the lost will be lost for eternity. The lost, I believe, will then see the divine genius of the plan of salvation – the wisdom of the cross – but it will then be too late. Forever too late! This, I believe, is what will make lostness unbearable. It will make Hell, Hell!

Imagine standing before the Judge of all the Universe on that final Day of Judgment and seeing nail prints in His wrists – nail prints that say that mankind, including you and me, really is lost after all! And *so* lost that it took God become Man to die for us. Imagine finally realizing that the truth is that "Nothing less than the death of God's Son on Calvary's cross could get the sinner into Heaven," and that "Nothing more than that was needed."[17] Imagine every lost son or daughter of Adam knowing that "Today I am going to prison forever, and ever, and ever, and ever, and ever...." And that "I could have been saved – that God passionately desired my being saved, that my salvation was totally paid for by Christ, and that I could have been living in Heaven's limitless bliss with my loving Creator and Savior for all eternity, but I said NO!" That "my eternal salvation cost God the most awesome price that could possibly be paid for ME and I turned *that* down!"

What kind of invitation have you been hearing? "Commit your life to God"? "Give your heart to Jesus"? "Repent, believe, and change your life"?

God says, "Christ died for sinners...believe on the Lord Jesus Christ and you will be saved."[18]

One invitation involves your "doing;" the other says that Christ did all your doing, and that the doing is all done! One involves your works, the other God's pure Grace. One brings delusion, the other salvation. Have you been "hat in hand" to Calvary where God always honors His Word?

The Bible clearly predicted that church history would be characterized by apostasy – departure from God and His Word. That Christians would exchange His truth for man's fables.[19] One thing you can count on: in a day of apostasy, even the leaders will "not walk uprightly according to the truth of the Gospel."[20]

Are you "outside the camp"[21] with our risen Christ proclaiming the message that He would be proclaiming if here, "Be reconciled to God"?[22] Be reconciled is written in the passive voice; the sinner *receives* the action of the verb, it is God who *performs* it. Have you done your homework going through the Pauline Epistles highlighting the things that were true of us when we were lost, and the things that became forever true of us the instant that we believed?

This is not a negative chapter; it is so positive that it should be making your heart jump up and click its heels. The Welshman Tommy Lawrence, Pastor, Bible teacher, and my *Romans* Professor at Barrington College, was preaching about the person and work of Christ in a New York rescue mission. An eleven year old boy, unable to contain his happiness, shouted, "HOT DOG!" Professor Lawrence treasured the memory of that little "Christ lover" and his quite appropriate response to the Gospel.

Ah, my friend, Almighty God, larger than the Universe that He created, Who lives before it, in it, out of it, above it, and beyond it, and Who one day will fold it up like a garment and lay it aside – exchanging it for a new one, extends to pipsqueak man the greatest invitation of all eternity. "Believe on the Lord Jesus Christ and YOU will be saved."[23] I find that most logical to believe and most wonderful to accept. And you?

CHAPTER TWELVE NOTES

1. Acts 16:30-31
2. Romans 4:4-5
3. Ephesians 2:8,9
4. Hebrews 1:3
5. Romans 5:12-21
6. Walter Wilson, M.D.
7. Galatians 2:20-21; Titus 3:5
8. Isaiah 64:6
9. John 19:28-30
10. John 14:6
11. Acts 16:31
12. Romans 6:23
13. Proverbs 1:7; 9:10
14. I Corinthians 3:18
15. I Corinthians 1:8
16. II Corinthians 6:2
17. Col. R.B. Thieme, Jr., USAF, Retired – Houston, TX
18. Romans 5:8; Acts 16:31
19. II Timothy 4:3-4
20. Galatians 2:14
21. Hebrews 13:13
22. II Corinthians 5:17-21
23. Acts 16:31

CHAPTER THIRTEEN

TWO WAYS

There are two ways to do God's work – God's way, or man's way. Someone said, "God's work, done in God's way will never lack for God's blessing." Someone else said, "I would rather fail at doing God's work in God's way than to succeed at doing God's work in my way."

We live in an age of compromise. Mega churches and super churches are springing up everywhere, organized on the concept of "making the gospel palatable." One pastor of a very large church told me that he would rather "give a little truth to a lot of people than give a lot of truth to a few." I thought of Paul when he said, "I have not shunned to declare to you the whole counsel of God," and "I have kept back nothing that is profitable for you."[1] God moved our Apostle Paul to declare, "If I still preach circumcision then is the offense of the cross ceased."[2] Had he continued to preach circumcision, he would have had much larger congregations.

The gospel can only be "made palatable" to the flesh by giving the flesh something to do. Strip a man of his imagined righteousness, take away his "doing," invite him to kneel empty-handed at a disgusting, offensive cross where God does everything, leaving nothing for man to do, and the challenge facing the super church crowd becomes insurmountable. Man, even Christian man, wants desperately to impress God by "doing" something for Him. It makes man feel good about himself; and after all, self-image has become the theme of much "ministry" today.

"Come to Christ; He wants you to be healthy, wealthy, and happy," is the siren song of many of today's Christian leaders and T.V. personalities. Luther, Wesley, and Whitefield drew crowds of twenty thousand without the benefit of a microphone, an auditorium or stadium, without rock music, a drama group, a girls' trio or a mens' ensemble. They were not always correct in what they said, but their emphasis was the Word of God, and they all recognized that believers are "called upon not only to believe on Him but to suffer for His name's sake."[3] The pastor of a church of many thousands was asked by a volunteer office worker, "Pastor, why don't you give the people Bible doctrine?" "Because they wouldn't come back," he answered. It doesn't seem to matter whether you preach in favor of Pentecostalism or against it, in favor of Calvinism or against it, as long as you replace the "unpalatable" Gospel of God's Grace with Lordship salvation and provide enough "different strokes for different folks;" it seems that you can draw the multitudes – and keep them coming.

The Philippian jailor asked Paul, "What must *I do* to be saved?" He was typical of man in the flesh who will accept a "gospel" that leaves room for "doing," room for impressing God. Just don't get man so totally lost, by your preaching, that he *cannot* impress God and has to be saved by "laying his deadly doing down," coming hat-in-hand to Calvary, and letting God do all the saving, while he does only all the being saved.

Remember, God doesn't save "diamonds in the rough." When Grace found you, you weren't a precious gemstone on your way to being cut, polished, and displayed in Tiffany's. You were on your way to Gehenna, the garbage dump of eternity. God isn't foolish; He doesn't send diamonds to the dump! You and I were on our way to Gehenna when Calvary intervened, saving us from our appointed, and well-deserved destiny. That doesn't make a person feel good about himself. I want to think well of myself as much as anyone, but my self-esteem had better be spiritual self-esteem. Spiritual self-esteem recognizes that, if we're diamonds, our first birth didn't make us so...it took a *second*!

The most important question that an unsaved person could ask is, "What must I do to be saved?"[4] The most important question one can ask after trusting Christ and God has saved him, is "Lord, what will you have me to do?"[5] Perhaps, in the final analysis, it is the most important, but it cannot be asked until the first question has been answered. The Westminster Shorter Catechism says, "The chief end [purpose] of man is to glorify God, and to enjoy Him forever." Those old Presbyterians got the meaning of life right, didn't they? God's indictment of man is, "They glorified Him not as God, neither were thankful."[6] True thankfulness can only come from a heart of rejoicing – a joyful heart; and it always results from glorifying God – from worshiping and serving the Creator, not the creature.

Do you want true happiness? If you seek it, you will never find it. If you seek to please God, the inevitable result will be that His joy will become yours.

The will of God is not the *worst* thing that can possibly happen to us, as our flesh greatly fears, but the *best* thing. No creature could possibly be happier than when kneeling before the throne of God. Worship is what you and I were designed for and we will never be truly content until it engulfs us, until it becomes the warp and woof of our thinking, the fabric of our being. "You shall worship the Lord your God, and Him only shall you serve."[7] Christ connected worship and service and "what God has joined together let not man put asunder." During my nineteen years on the radio, many listeners called inquiring about the sponsoring Church, Grace Gospel Fellowship, and asking, "Do you worship?" I always wondered, "Do you serve?"

If we would serve God in God's way, we must recognize that much that is called service is not serving God, but serving ourselves. If we are "serving God" so that He won't give us "a flat tire, on a country road, in a rainstorm, at night," we are not really serving His best interests but our own. The same holds true if we are "serving God" to get a bigger house on a wider street in Heaven. If the "reward" that we seek is not that *He* may be glorified, we serve ourselves, not God. We cannot serve two masters. To really serve, the believer must abandon the self-life.

I cannot be saved by "giving my heart to Jesus;" no one ever has been and no one ever will be. *After* I am saved I can, and should, present myself – heart and all – to God as alive from the dead. Presenting myself must start with the "heart" if it is to end with the "all." Attitude produces action. If you would serve God in God's way, guard your attitude.... "Guard your heart, with all diligence, for out of it are the well-springs of life."[8]

"Only one life, 'twill soon be past.
Only what's done for Christ will last."

Christ connected worship and service, life and ministry. When I speak and when I write, it is very difficult for me to mention the Christian life without also mentioning Christian ministry. For instance, if I say, "God has made a perfect provision for every believer's life," ought I not add, "and ministry"? "God has made a perfect provision for every believer's life and ministry."

My life, with its interests, should never come before God and His interests. If my life becomes paramount, my life becomes my god. This is idolatry!

Should my ministry assume priority over my worship, it can also become a "god." The more "success" that accompanies ministry, the greater the temptation to put ministry where only Christ belongs. A ministry can turn into a business. The battlefield is strewn with the corpses of men who started out running well until *what* they were doing became more important than *why* they were doing it, and for *Whom* they were doing it.

A church may be growing by the thousands, with money coming in by the millions, and the pastor's image spreading far and wide without the pastor and the congregation realizing that God has been given a back seat. It is very hard for man to recognize that so much "success" can actually be failure.

No one has ever been saved by works. To present my works to God for the whole or even a part of my salvation is to reject the work of the Son of God upon the cross of Calvary.[9] Having been saved, however, makes my works – done God's way – well-pleasing to Him.[10] I am to live in a realm, or sphere, of good works.[11] I should study God's Word daily to know God's will. I should pray daily, first for the desire and then for the determination to do His will.

Philippians 2:13 says, "For it is God who works in you to will and to do of His good pleasure." The Greek verb "to will" means "to desire, purpose, plan." The meaning of the verb "to do" is self-evident.

The verb "to work" in "it is God who works in you..." is the verb "to operate." God wants to carry on an operation in us, and He wants to see it through from its inception to its culmination – from our desiring to our doing. This is Christian life. Anything less is other! Find a need in your local assembly or in the world around you that you can meet, and meet it. At times, we must cultivate a desire to do what we do not enjoy doing. Meeting needs is not always a pleasant occupation. Calvary met our greatest need, but the cross was far from enjoyable for Christ. Infinitely far.

Christian life and ministry begin within the believer's heart. Life and ministry are divine productions. They are not a work of the flesh, but a fruit or result of the indwelling of the Spirit of God. True success in ministry, as in life, depends on the power of Christ within. In salvation, Grace accomplishes what Law could not. This is equally true in life and ministry. The Christian life is a life lived in *total* dependence upon God. True prayer always recognizes this dependence. We must pray daily, hourly where possible, for a consuming passion to please God. Pray, and never quit praying that your desire may be an ever-increasing, an overwhelming, a never slackening desire to "do always those things that please Him."

When I decide to view ministry as a very large and integral part of life itself; to view life and ministry as inseparable parts of a whole, lesser decisions become simpler, though not always easier. Remember, for believers, the *degree of difficulty* is never our bottom line. The bottom line is always the *extent of supply*, and God is the one supplying! The very power of Heaven, resurrection power, is always available to us. Not the power to become healthy, wealthy, and happy, but the power to please God in all that we do. We don't mean to suggest that health, wealth, and happiness should be avoided, nor even neglected, but that they should never be our priority. We are not our own, we have been "bought with a price."[12] God is our priority. God!

Our service to God must always be a result of our appreciation for His saving, keeping Grace – never an attempt to pay Him back.

An eternity of serving could not pay for one minute in Heaven. That minute was purchased by the death of God's Son. If Mother Theresa is in Heaven, it is not because she went to Calcutta, but because God went to Calvary! If we could pay God back for some of it, we could, in time, pay Him back for all of it, but we can't pay Him back for any of it. Your salvation and mine was purchased at infinite cost to God – the life of His Son. But it *was* purchased and fully paid for. We can't pay for it in whole or in part – but we can appreciate it. Because *Christ* is the infinite price God paid, our salvation can be – must be – absolutely free to us. "Grace is all that God is free to do for you because of the death of His Son on the cross!"[13]

Our Apostle did not serve God to avoid a flat tire in time, nor to receive a mansion in eternity, nor to "pay God back" in the least. The love of Christ displayed at Calvary was Paul's sole motive for serving.[14] It was all that was needed to drive him ever onward, his love responding to the love from Christ on Calvary. "He that spared not His own Son, but delivered Him up for us all, how shall He not with Him also freely give us all things?"[15] How can we not respond to such a love as that? I hate to mention our love for Him in the same breath with His love for us. Our love at its best will always be a pitiful response to "His great love with which He loved us,"[16] and it could not be otherwise. Our attempts to show our gratitude for all that He is and does are most feeble in time. In eternity, our realization of the magnitude of divine love will call forth all that lies within us. It will still be a pittance, though it be all that we are and have.

Never again will we have the awesome challenge that is ours now: to give up our all to Him in this great conflict of the ages. If we love Him, we will forego "the pleasures of sin [that are] for a season,"[17] to love Him back with all that we can be and all that we can do. We must depend on the indwelling Holy Spirit for this. The resources of Heaven are ours – the power of Christ within.

CHAPTER THIRTEEN NOTES

1. Acts 20:20,27
2. Galatians 5:11
3. Philippians 1:29
4. Acts 16:30
5. Acts 9:6
6. Romans 1:21
7. Matthew 4:10
8. Proverbs 4:23
9. Galatians 2:19-21
10. Titus 3:8
11. Ephesians 2:8-10
12. I Corinthians 6:19-20
13. Col. R.B. Thieme, Jr., USAF, Retired – Houston, TX
14. II Corinthians 5:14-15
15. Romans 8:32
16. Ephesians 2:4-5
17. Hebrews 11:25

CHAPTER FOURTEEN

TWO GOALS

God's Word says in Philippians 2:13 that, "...it is God which worketh in you both to will and to do of His good pleasure. Then, I Corinthians 3: 10-15 tells us that the goal of the Christian life is "...to will and to do those things that are pleasing in His sight." They are not always pleasing in our sight, but pleasing ourselves is not a proper goal for believers; it is a disease! One day you will put your big toe on Heaven's shore, and from that moment on, you will "do always those things that please Him." You and I have never done that. So far, only Christ has consistently and uninterruptedly done the perfect will of the Father. Imagine, never once displeasing God for all of eternity. Ever, ever again! But we're not there yet! Right now we are to desire to do the will of God, purpose to do His will, and plan how to do it. We cannot do it perfectly yet, but, in dependence upon the power of Christ within, we can enjoy an ever-increasing amount of success. I can pray daily, hourly, that I may desire what God desires yet more and more. As prayer grows, desire blossoms, and the fruit will surely be occupation with Christ and the plan He has for me.

Bible study is the believer's number one priority. If "the chief end of man is to glorify God,"[1] I must learn from God just how to do this. A Bible that I can't understand is of no more profit than a Bible I do not have. To understand the Bible I must follow the "rules" of Bible understanding.

Unlimited Grace

What do I know about these few verses in Corinthians? Well, they were written to correct errors already existing in the early church. They are written by God and Paul – the sole Apostle for the Body of Christ. The Twelve are Apostles to Israel and to the Gentiles to whom Israel is to be "a kingdom of priests" in the future, her program having been interrupted when she refused God and Peter's offer of the return of the King. When that happened, God intercalated an unprophesied "Dispensation of Grace," in which the Body of Christ – not Israel – is center stage. This Dispensation, or economy, will continue until God recalls His ambassadors from Planet Earth through the miracle of the Rapture. Then He will reach down, restart His prophetic clock, and resume dealing with the world through His favored nation, Israel. Right now, Heaven has but one Apostle to Earth, Paul, and we are to follow him as he follows Christ. One could not follow God in the economy of Law without following Moses, and one cannot follow Christ today unless one follows Paul. Don't make too much of Paul. Don't make too little of him either!

The Twelve Apostles, while not ours, are still important. Three of them wrote Scripture. God employed them to produce only eight books, but those books are part of God's Word and, as such, are *for* us, though not *to* us nor *about* us. While ALL of the Word is FOR us, one thirteenth of the Bible is TO us and ABOUT us and God chose our Apostle to write those fourteen books.

Another key to understanding this passage is to recognize that I Corinthians is an Acts period book. During the Acts period, God was still dealing with Israel as a nation even though the Kingdom offer had been refused by Israel and withdrawn by God, and the Dispensation of Grace had begun. This means that some things related to Israel and her program were still going on and would only cease with the setting aside of Israel.[2]

The confusion arises when this section is preached as a post-Rapture judgment of all members of the Body. The subject is teachers and what they teach. The teachers and the students are clearly distinguished and the "judgment" is of the teachers, not the students. The Bema Seat is not mentioned, nor is it in view.

Remember the key of *context*? The basic problem in the churches of Corinth was subscription to human viewpoint in preference to divine viewpoint. The first four chapters deal with this problem, and the rest of the book with the consequences of choosing man's logic over God's. The vaunted intellectualism of the Corinthians was second only to that of the Athenians. But being first or second in the foolishness of man is no substitute for agreeing with the genius of God! They may have been giants in philosophy – the speculations of man – but they were infants in theology – the science of God. The results of their humanism included partisanship, sectarianism, fighting, competing, legalism, arrogance, drunkenness, heresy, and sexual immorality.

We either listen to God or Satan. Turning from light leaves man with only darkness. There was a preference for the impressive oratory of Apollos over the simple, direct teaching of Paul. Paul humbly reminds his converts that, in the economy of God, he was to plant the seed, Apollos' job was to water what Paul had planted, and God would give the harvest. Then, switching metaphors, he reminds them that God had made the choice of Paul to be the master architect and Apollos one of the builders. Anyone who built on the architect's foundation must follow the blueprint meticulously. Today, as then, men mix a little of Paul with a little of Moses and come up with a lot of disaster! The "grace of God given to me" was a reference to Paul's unique apostleship and distinctive message.

Since the foundation is doctrinal and spiritual the superstructure must be as well. If anyone, any teacher, build on God and Paul's foundation, he must use Pauline materials – Pauline doctrine. Apollos, and today's preachers and teachers as well, must water the seed that Paul has planted! The "judgment" in this passage, like that in Hebrews 13:17, is an assessment of teachers and their teaching, not all believers and their works. Almost invariably when commentators deal with the judgment in this passage they point out that "this is not a judgment of the believer's sins, but of his works." They then go on to pronounce against fornication. Isn't fornication a sin as well as a work?

Every Scripture must be taken seriously. While this is not a passage warning against *sexual* immorality – other verses do that – it warns against *spiritual* immorality, the immorality of building on God and Paul's foundation with non-Pauline materials, such as instructions for other believers in other dispensations that conflict with our message from Heaven.

CHAPTER FOURTEEN NOTES

1. Westminster Shorter Catechism
2. Acts 28:25-28

CHAPTER FIFTEEN

A THOUSAND OAKS

Cujo stretched out in solid comfort on the deck, his fawn colored fur soaking up the morning sun. Five stories above him, in a six story oak, a mischievous squirrel released an acorn with remarkable accuracy. It plummeted Earthward striking the big Doberman dead center above and between his eyebrows. Cujo rose like a rocket, whirled like a dervish, and, fangs bared, glared angrily aloft. His eyes searched the branches above him for the unerring bombardier. It wasn't the first bombing; it wouldn't be the last.

Locked in that little acorn were a thousand oaks, or perhaps a thousand generations of oaks. Our ancestor Adam was created perfect but volitional; he had the power of choice. He chose rebellion, and you and I were locked in his loins when he sinned, and fell, and died a spiritual death. An acorn produces after its kind and so does a human. An acorn never produces a watermelon, a diamond, or an elephant. It produces an oak. Always. Only. Fallen, rebellious Adam could only produce fallen, rebellious humans. A fallen race was stored in his gene pool.

When Adam fell, he fell all the way. He didn't catch his blue jeans on a branch half way down. He didn't hit bottom and bounce up. He fell all the way into spiritual death, into a totally lost condition. If your church, in its preaching, never gets you totally lost, demand your money back. We didn't start life bent, but broken, not sick but dead, not in need of a second chance but hell-bound and hell-deserving. Christ would not have gone to the cross to save us from anything less than complete ruin, nor would His loving Father have sent Him there.

The Fall of man explains why our history is written in blood, why we need courts and police officers, and armies and navies, and why we have created newer, faster ways to kill each other. Every time you drive past a hospital, mental health facility, jail, battlefield, or cemetery, God and history are telling you that the human race is a lost race, and you are a lost person. Both as a race and as individuals we need a Savior. Thank God that He anticipated our need in eternity past. "The Lamb was slain from the foundation of the World."[1]

God knew light years before we were born that you and I would need a Savior and He provided one. Just one. Not a thousand, a hundred, a dozen, or even two. Just one.[2] The *only* one. Why? Because only one could qualify to bring an infinitely Holy God and totally ruined sinners together, and because only one was needed. The cross is God's way of bringing man to Himself. Don't try to understand it, because you can't. Just believe it. Nearly everything we have good reason to believe we cannot understand. I don't understand food, nor does anyone else, but we consume food every day.

It was a Tuesday morning late in April. I awoke to a bright, sunny day sheltered by a cheerfully blue sky studded with little cotton-puff clouds hurrying from somewhere to nowhere as though their lives depended on it. This was the first time I had ever arisen as a new creature with a new nature derived from a new birth. Wow! Monday morning the old Jimmy had gotten up believing that the solar system revolved around Jim. Tuesday morning was different. The new Jim arose seeming to know intuitively that the solar system, even the Universe, revolves around Christ. Some other things seemed different too. The Sun seemed brighter, the sky bluer, the grass greener, and the flowers more beautiful as I headed off to work. One thing disturbed me. When new Jimmy looked in the mirror to shave, what looked strangely like old Jimmy stared back. Oh well, it really didn't matter after all. I had gone to bed knowing for the first time in my life, where I will spend eternity, feeling "sheltered safe within the arms of God." I understood one thing: that I had been lost and now was found; that someone loved me intensely and that that someone was the Creator of the Universe.

How lost were you? Remember, we didn't become lost when we sinned our first sin with cognizance. The sin that made us lost was the sin of the race. It took place long ago in Adam's garden. Adam committed it, but we participated in it. Adam, the individual sinned – so did Adam, the race (mankind). When the acorn fell, all the acorns fell, generations of acorns. When Adam fell, we fell. When he sinned, we sinned. When he died spiritually, we died spiritually.

One "little" sin plunged the entire human race into total ruin. We are so completely ruined that it took God dying in our place to save us. Why? Because the "one little sin" was not little! It was a declaration of war against the Creator by the creature! Against an all-loving Creator by a now hate-filled created being. The war in Heaven fought by Satan and his fallen angels against God and His holy Angels was now joined by a war on Earth, a war against God by fallen Adam and his fallen progeny.

Would God sweep the acorns into the fireplace and start over again, or would He take old acorns and make them new? You can't know who you are and why you're here until you know where you came from and where you're going! You don't have to go to India and help a naked fat man study the lint in his navel to discover the meaning of life. Come to Calvary– bring the fat man with you.

Our Apostle Paul understood the purpose of life because he knew that *old* Paul was justly condemned and that *new* Paul was graciously justified – moved forever beyond the reach of condemnation. Another had assumed his condemnation bearing the wrath of God as Paul's substitute. Another had paid his bill in full, and God never collects a debt twice!

Churches that don't get us all the way lost never get us all the way saved. If you're in one, choose Christ over church. If we choose church over Christ, we dishonor God and declare our own imbecility!

There have been many April evenings since I trusted Christ alone for my salvation. There have been many April mornings since I first realized that a Christ worth trusting is a Christ worth loving – and worth living for. In the early days of my Christian life, I frequently fell asleep on my knees at my bedside, my face resting on the tear-stained pages of my Bible. I would read of Calvary where God forever proved His infinite love for His enemies – for totally ruined sinners – for you and me!

God's love is not demonstrated by your circumstances. He never says, "Look how healthy, wealthy, and happy you are. Doesn't that prove that I love you?" We may be ill, broke, and unhappy tomorrow. That's life! No, God always points us to the cross to prove the reality and the measure of His love. This all-important fact is too often missing from today's preaching. We need, you and I, to get back to our tear-stained Bibles – stained with tears of sorrow that *our* sins made *His* cross necessary, and tears of gratitude and joy that He loves us that much.

When a well known major league pitcher trusted Christ in an evangelistic meeting, the evangelist told the world to watch the pitcher have his most successful season now that he was a believer. He didn't. He had his worst, and soon slipped through the cracks of fame to be lost in the dark night of oblivion. Trusting Christ cost the Apostle Paul family, friends, position, wealth, worldly security, and physical well-being, not to mention freedom, and life itself. His unique Apostolic ministry was characterized by frequent hunger, thirst, exposure, discouragement, rejection, beatings, jailings, shipwrecks, betrayals, and finally loss of his earthly life. But the pitcher and the Apostle received eternal life as a gratuitous gift, bought and fully paid for by God's Son on His cross. Did all the "stuff" that followed their salvation really matter? No. "Stuff" never matters. Have we learned that?

You and I are acorns, too. Acorns that came from an original acorn. Acorns with a thousand oaks stored in us. Lost acorns that can only produce lost oaks. All of our descendants, like us and our ancestors, will spend eternity saved or lost. How serious we are about Christ and how positive we are toward Bible doctrine, may incline our progeny to trust Christ and be eternally saved, or to reject Him and be eternally lost. They, too, will influence their children for God and eternal salvation or for sin and eternal damnation in Gehenna, the garbage dump of forever!

Do you see how important you are in the scheme of things, in the very serious drama of Grace being played out in time on Earth? When I was a sixteen year old working my way through high school, I worked nights at Underwood Typewriter Company. In our department, there was a man named Acorn. Everyone else had a first name, but he was only known as "Acorn." He was the man nobody knew; he never spoke to anyone and we gave up on speaking to him. He was just "Acorn," except that no one is "just Acorn." Everyone, even those who bring no children into the world, influences others toward Heaven or toward Hell. As believers, we must learn to season our speech with grace, that we may plant, or perhaps water, a seed that God can nurture and eventually harvest for Heaven. Serious business, this being an acorn! We influence others, generations of others, toward Calvary – or away from it.

The Galatians trusted the Grace message and were eternally saved. God only saves eternally. Then, as quickly as they had turned *to* Grace, they turned *from* it. This did not cost them their salvation – salvation is forever, but it cost many generations of their children *their* salvation because they bequeathed to their children a wrong example and a wrong message.

Think about that, Mr. Acorn!

CHAPTER FIFTEEN NOTES

1. Revelation 13:8
2. John 14:6; I Timothy 2:5; Acts 4:12

CHAPTER SIXTEEN

LEARNING TO LIVE

~

Grace is your teacher. Mine too. God and Paul tell us, "For the Grace of God appeared which brings salvation for all men, instructing us that, having denied active irreverence and worldly passions, we should live sensibly, and uprightly, and reverently in this present age, awaiting the blessed hope and appearing of the glory of our great God and Savior Jesus Christ, who gave Himself for us, that He might redeem us from all lawlessness, and might purify to Himself a special people, zealous of good works."[1]

Here God and Paul identify Christ as "our Great God and Savior." Modern Arians will attempt to rob us of this tremendous and all-important truth by positing two people here. One "Great God," and the other "Savior." The Greek language in which this was originally written, does not permit this. Remember, God never wrote a word in English. There are two nouns but only one definite article, one "the." This requires the reader to understand that the two nouns, "God" and "Savior," represent one Person; Christ is both "Great God" and "Savior." This is one of many statements in Scripture that clearly declare the absolute deity of Christ. Christ is God! The wonder of our salvation is that Almighty God became a man – without ceasing to be God – and walked the Earth for a third of a century with His face set as a flint toward Calvary. God became man that He might die in the place of man, bearing man's sins and so effecting reconciliation between God and man.[2]

To put one hand on God's shoulder and one hand on man's and bring the two together, the redeemer had to be both God and man. It's that simple! Only one Person in the Universe fills that bill. There is only one God-Man in all of eternity, our Lord Jesus Christ. There are not several, not even two. Just one! Man may invent co-redeemers or redemptresses, but God and His Word plainly limit us to one – the only one who could qualify. God became a man to die for sinners. The once-for-ever death of God the Son completely satisfied the offended holiness of God the Father. No, Christ didn't just throw the door of Heaven open, making it possible for man to save himself with the help of religion. Christ saves "to the uttermost all that come to God through Him." "To the uttermost" can only mean completely and eternally.[3]

If your church teaches a salvation that isn't complete and eternal – walk! God's purpose in providing a pastor-teacher is to bring us to spiritual maturity by teaching us the "epignosis" of Christ. Gnosis is knowledge; Epignosis is full knowledge, advanced knowledge, college-level knowledge of the Person and work of God, our Savior Jesus Christ. If a pastor doesn't understand phase one: salvation, how can he teach phase two: life and ministry? If he hasn't been brought to maturity, how can he bring you to maturity? Never stop loving him or his people, thank him sincerely for who he is and for what he has done for you. Don't undermine his ministry, and don't split his church. Walk, Brother, walk! Walk, Sister, walk! God's will regarding your spiritual maturity, clearly revealed in Scripture, cannot be ignored without a lifetime of willful disobedience on your part.[4]

Every morning, when you and I open our eyes on a new 24-hour slice of opportunity, we must ask ourselves, "Am I going to do God's will today or my own will?" Your old sin nature is Christ's greatest rival, and your worst enemy! If your church, peer group, or tradition is coming between God and you, you have a choice to make, don't you? Hard choices become easier when we put Christ first. Are you putting Christ first? Did you get up this morning deciding to sacrifice your will on the altar of His?

Romans 8:31 asks, "If God is for us, who can be against us?" The success motivation crowd twists this to mean that since God is "on our side," we can sell more insurance, real estate or used cars.

The health, wealth, and happiness gospelers suggest that God being for us means that He rules out adversity for people of "faith." Others teach that God's taking our part means that Grandma will recover from the effects of her fall, sonny will be kept safe on his motorcycle, and darling daughter will eventually stop sharing her apartment with unemployed drug-heads and "return to God," perhaps when she is old.

But the God of Romans eight means much more than this, and much more than this means much *other* than this. God is for us, but life isn't pain-free. One may be in the center of God's will and life may still be pain-full!

God being for us means that "[our] sins, which are many, are all washed away." Romans 8:31 means that the God who erased the believer's blackboard is the God who threw the blackboard away. It teaches us that the only God who can erase blackboards and throw them away is worth the love of heart, soul, mind, and strength – always!

Let's take a new look at our old text. It begins with "The grace of God" and ends with our "good works." Thus it is, thus be it ever! God's Grace must always do its complete work before we can do our works. Salvation, life, and ministry not only begin with Grace but consist in Grace throughout from beginning to end, time to eternity. Our works are never "the means of Grace." The only means of Grace is Calvary, and Calvary *alone*.[5] "Grace is all that God is free to do for you because of the death of His Son on the cross!"[6] Good works on our part NEVER produce Grace on God's part. Your works and mine can never merit unmerited favor. We can never deserve undeserved kindness.

The original Biblical text says literally, "For the Grace of God appeared which brings salvation for all people."[7] Christ wept over those in Jerusalem who, down through the centuries, He so often "would have gathered" but "[they] would not." The problem, then as now, was not that they were not elect and so *could* not be gathered, but that when He *would,* they *wouldn't.* All who believe the salvation message are divinely placed in union with Christ, who Himself is elect from eternity past, thus we become members of the elect by sharing in His election. All "whosoevers" who believe *become* included in election. Christ didn't weep for the elect, the "whosoever woulds," there was no need to. He wept for the "whosoever wouldn'ts" who were offered life and turned it down. Are you a "whosoever will" or a "whosoever won't"?

Verse 12 says, "...instructing us that, having denied active irreverence and worldly passions, we should live sensibly, uprightly, and reverently in this present age." Saving Grace is for all men, but it can only teach "us," the saved. Salvation is available for all; instruction (lit. "child training") is only for God's children. Are you God's child? If you are, this instruction is for you.

First comes salvation where God does all the saving and we do only all the being saved! Then, having been saved, we deny our active irreverence (overt), and worldly passions (covert).

There *is* a lifestyle to be rejected by *every* believer. It is a lifestyle of inner attitudes and outer actions emanating from the old sin nature and incompatible with God's plan for our lives. Law reveals the corruption of the very nature of man.[8] Grace brings with it a totally new nature that responds to the revealed will of God in Scripture.

> "Do this and live, the Law commands,
> but gives me neither feet nor hands.
> A better word the Gospel brings;
> it bids me fly and gives me wings!"

Grace not only "child trains" us to deny irreverence and worldly cravings, but to live responsibly, properly, and devotedly in these challenging times. But Grace teaches even more. It teaches us to anticipate eagerly the happy prospect of Christ's certain return to translate His ambassadors from Earth to Heaven *before* the war in Heaven and the war on Earth become one. Then we shall enjoy the glorious appearing of "our Great God and Savior Christ Jesus."

Paul, taught by Grace, loved the teaching of the Rapture of the Church and also that of the return of Christ. He also never tired of the good news of our salvation and its results in our lives, yours and mine.

One of the reasons for Christ giving Himself to that cruel and criminal cross, redeeming us, is that He might purify to Himself a peculiar (lit. "treasured") people who would be "zealous of good works." If you've been to Calvary and trusted Christ, my friend, you're special. God "treasures" you; think of it! Grace takes Earth's garbage and converts it into Heaven's treasure!

Grace appears bringing salvation, then teaching the saved to live for Christ in eager anticipation of our certain destiny.

In chapter three, verse eight, we have the same order; God's Grace, *then* our works. The order is always the same. "Keep on affirming strongly that those *having believed* God may take care to be aggressive in [doing] good works."

Wow!

CHAPTER SIXTEEN NOTES

1. Titus 2:11-14
2. Romans 5:11
3. Hebrews 7:25
4. Ephesians 4:11-16
5. I Corinthians 1:8
6. Col. R.B. Thieme, Jr., USAF, Retired – Houston, TX
7. Titus 2:11
8. Romans 3:20

CHAPTER SEVENTEEN

WHY CHURCH?

Who needs a pastor? Everybody! Says who? Says God![1] Millions of Christians have no church to attend, no local assembly, and no pastor. Perhaps they live in Muslim countries, or communist countries, where real churches and real pastors are frowned on and even outlawed – where Christians are punished, tortured, or killed. Some of these Christians, of necessity, find their "local assembly" on T.V., radio, the internet, or other media. Hopefully, it's a Gospel preaching and ideally, a rightly dividing assembly.

There are also millions of professing Christians who live within an easy commute from a group of Bible believing Christians, but fail to attend their meetings regularly because, frankly, God and His Word are not their number one priority. But God designed the local assembly for *you*, and *you* for the local assembly. Something is seriously wrong when a believer is not where God would have him be, doing what God would have him do. Don't count on things going right if you're going wrong. God has a plan for every believer; He has a plan for *you*.

God's plan for the believer's life and ministry includes not only regular attendance at a good local assembly, but a fierce loyalty to that assembly growing out of an overwhelming devotion to Christ. Our love for God can always be measured by our love for His Word. If you have caught God's drumbeat, you will be thrilled by what He says to you in Ephesians 4:11-16. "And He [Christ] gave some...

shepherds and teachers." The use of "kai" ("and") is ascensive, not adjunctive. That is, it means "shepherds *even* teachers;" shepherds *who are* teachers, not shepherds *plus* teachers. The Holy Spirit is here describing one office or function, not two. "Teachers" is emphatic in the original Greek, and God never wrote a word in English! The Christ who gave Apostles, prophets, evangelists, and shepherds who are teachers to the "assembly which is His body," (that includes you and me), is the Christ who made eternity's longest journey from Heaven's throne to Earth's cross and back to Heaven's throne.[2]

Everything that the God-Man does is important! He is not the God of the unimportant, and the provision of the office and function of the shepherd-teacher is important – vitally important to you and to me. This divine provision involves God's plan for the believer's life and ministry. Never say, "Christian life" without adding "and ministry" because a life without a ministry is a meaningless life! God's plan for our lives begins with our becoming saints (v. 12), but doesn't end there. He means for us to go on to "perfection"– completion, maturity or "readiness for service"; the service being building up of the Body of Christ. Unsaved people cannot do work that God has designed for saved people (saints) to do.

I read an internet printout from the Vatican Library on the subject of assurance of salvation. The anonymous author said that when Paul wrote his letter to the Church of Rome (Romans), he addressed it to "saints," not because he believed that all of the Roman believers *were* saints, but in the hope that "one or two of them might *become* saints." Bible passages that prove beyond dispute that every saved person is a saint are numerous, and consulting an exhaustive concordance on the use of the word "saint" will enable you to demonstrate this comforting truth to yourself. "Saint" simply means "set apart one" and, in context, "set apart by salvation." In the Epistles, all believers are called saints by God Himself, and are said to be "sanctified," or "saint-ified" in Christ.

We begin our sainthood as babies and we need to develop in order to grow. The goal is full maturity which cannot be realized in an absolute sense in this lifetime, but the privilege and responsibility of every believer, every saint, is constant growth, uninterrupted progress toward that goal. "If you aim at nothing, you'll hit it every time!" The average believer aims at nothing for a lifetime... and hits it! Don't be average. Average is never God's will for any believer. Spiritual life is always and only supernatural life, and supernatural life is never average or ordinary.

How long did God intend for His gift of shepherd-teacher to be available? The 13th verse tells us "until we all may arrive at the unity of the faith, even of the advanced knowledge of the Son of God...." That means until the job is done! Until we *all* are spiritually mature regarding a college-level understanding of the person and work of Christ. The regular intake of sound (in the Greek it's "healthy") Bible doctrine can move us from infancy to maturity. When we understand what we study and apply it to daily life we grow and great things happen to us that improve life, worship, and service.

Babies are wonderful. But babies were designed to grow up; spiritual babies too. Grow, man, grow! It's the name of the game! In verse 14, the Ephesians were told to no longer be infants, and neither should you and I. Spiritual babies aren't able to stand for anything, but they sure can fall for everything. A radio listener once called to complain that her teenage son was involved in a cult, and she wanted to know what to do about it. I made several suggestions, but first I asked her in what denomination she had raised him. It was an apostate church that soft-pedaled the deity of our Lord and denied the Bible's prescription for salvation. I pointed out that she and her church had not prepared her son to resist the evil winds of "systematized error." If our little boats are driven by the divine wind – "carried along" by the Holy Spirit's breath – the Word of God, we will not only *survive* life, but *triumph* in it. Otherwise we are headed for shipwreck! Did this mother herself know the Lord? I don't know, but if she did she chose her church and her pastor for all the wrong reasons.

Picking a church because it's close to home, brick instead of frame, stone instead of brick, because Grandpa helped build it, our family has always attended it, it is old, large, or popular just doesn't cut it with Scripture! Not even with common sense! You and I need an assembly that will incline us to embrace the truth, "In love to grow up into Him in all things; [Him] who is the Head – the Christ. From whom [Christ] all the body, joined and united by every transfer point of supply according to the operating in its measure of every single part, makes increase of the body to the building up of itself in love."[3]

The intake of sound Bible doctrine is the believer's number one priority. In God's ideal plan, the local assembly is the primary source of sound Bible doctrine. Ideally, every child should have a father, a mother, and a pastor. The pastor is God's gift to believers. The pastor should lead where he can, and rule where he must. When the sheep strays from the flock, it strays from the shepherd. My pastor once said to me, "God sure knew what He was doing when He gave the shepherd's rod to the shepherd and not to the sheep." Congregational government is a myth. One strong willed individual runs every congregation that seeks to practice it. "The strong willed are usually wrong willed," to quote my pastor, John Kirkwood. People who object to the shepherd as governor will always sit still for, or even actively support, some male or female power-freak governing the church with their carnal mind. God's plan is that the shepherd should do the shepherding, using the shepherd's rod, his God-given authority, where necessary. A church that can't abide this divine provision should have elected the power-freak as pastor in the first place. The shepherd's rod is Scripture, rightly divided and lovingly, though firmly applied.

The pastor teaches "with a view to the perfecting of the saints."[4] The goal of the teacher and the taught is perfection, completeness, "full readiness," an accomplished end resulting from a process – spiritual maturity for worship and service. Nothing must be allowed to *distract* from the attainment of this goal. This goal is God's goal for every saint – for you and me. That's why we must live every day with dedicated focus. Do you have the eye of the tiger? Do you want to?

We are not saved by serving, as all religions teach, but we are saved to serve. God saved us that His glory – what is true of Him – might be revealed in His Grace. He saved us also that He might display His power in winning the angelic conflict. In addition, He saved us because of His great love for us. Then, too, He saved us that we might realize our proper destiny, that of worshiping and serving Him.

Service requires a degree of maturity. The degree of our spiritual maturity determines the level of our service. "Never send a boy to do a man's job." Gertrude Crane was the mother of the Reed boys, Tommy and Norval, two of my best friends. Just weeks after I was saved, she trusted Christ in a street meeting. The next day I went to see her and the boys. They were home, but she had taken a shoe box full of gospel tracts that I had left there and gone all alone to pass them out in front of a large downtown theatre. Saved less than 24 hours, she knew intuitively that saints, even brand new saints, were designed to serve their Savior. She wanted to, and she did!

The service in view in our text is "building up of the body of Christ." Are you building up or tearing down? "He that gathers not with me scatters abroad."[5]

Verse 13 tells us that the office of shepherd-teacher will continue until the Rapture, until the job is done. The Greek verb "to shepherd" means "to tend" the sheep. Another Greek verb means "to feed." Christ used both words when He had asked Peter, "Do you love me?" The sheep of God's fold can only be fed and tended by the teaching of God's Word. Most "pastors" aren't essentially teachers. All are supposed to be. Sheep must be fed and tended. It's as simple as that!

God hasn't commissioned pastors to build large churches, "make the Gospel palatable," devise programs for everyone or replace the Bible as the believer's counselor. Pastoring a large church doesn't make a man a failure, but only feeding and tending sheep can make him a success. Jim Jones had a "church" of thirty-thousand. Noah had only seven... all relatives. Which was the failure and which the success?

The unity of believers must be doctrinal unity, not sentimental. God is a thinker, not a feeler. He calls us to think with Him. God wants His people united, not denominated, not denominationalized, but the unity God calls for is on the *basis* of the faith, not at the *expense* of the faith. Man says, "let's dispense with doctrine so that we can all be one." God says that we are all to be one by all believing the same thing – the Grace message of the risen, glorified Christ, sometimes called the Pauline message. It is not called "Pauline" because it is a product of Paul's genius. It is the genius of God, which He has chosen to communicate through Paul.

Doctrine (sound Bible teaching) is the foundation for life and ministry. "It is not in man who walks to direct his steps."[7] If you want to *go* right, you must know what *is* right. Doctrinal unity, the goal, can only come through a college-level knowledge of the person and work of Jesus Christ. Christ is the ultimate shepherd both of Israel and of the Body of Christ. All other shepherds are under-shepherds and must get their directions from Him. Superchurch pastors, with their policy of compromising God's Word by "making the Gospel palatable" to the unsaved, are not doing this.

Christ, in claiming to be "the Good Shepherd," was claiming the absolute deity of the Shepherd of Psalm 23. The God-Man is the Shepherd, and we are the sheep. Remembering this self-evident truth guards us against the popular self-idolatry of our day, "you shall be as God."

Verse 14 plainly and powerfully shows that willful babyhood is contrary to God's expressed will, and therefore not an option for the saint.

Verse 15 is the solution to the problems of verse 14. We are to "embrace" the truth... to hug the daylights out of it and never stop hugging. Grace truth is not an addendum to life, but life itself. "Doctrine is the stuff that life is made of," because Christ alone is "The Way, The Truth, and The Life."[8]

There must be steady progress from spiritual infancy to spiritual maturity. Anything less than this is *NOT* the Christian life. Anything less is something other!

CHAPTER SEVENTEEN NOTES

1. Hebrews 10:24-25
2. Ephesians 4:8-10 ; Philippians 2:5-11
3. Ephesians 4:15,16
4. Ephesians 4:12
5. Matthew 12:30
6. I Corinthians 1:10
7. Jeremiah 10:23
8. John 14:6

CHAPTER EIGHTEEN

SEATED WITH CHRIST

How saved is saved? Am I completely and eternally saved, or could sin or unbelief "unsave" me? Am I forever safely clutched in the clenched fist of God the Father and of God the Son or am I on probation?[1] Is there anything that exists now, or ever could exist that is powerful enough to undo the crosswork of Christ where it concerns me?[2] Is my salvation totally God's work for me, or is it, in whole or in part, my work for Him?[3] In short, can a saved person ever be lost?

This is one of the most frequently asked questions on Christian call-in radio programs. There probably has not been one minute in church history when this question was not being asked, debated, or fought over; and this in spite of the fact that the answer is clear and simple and to be found everywhere in the Pauline Epistles for the last 2000 years.

The arguments raised against eternal salvation[4] evaporate when the rules of context and of original language are observed. On the other hand, the great texts that teach eternal salvation are unchallenged by following the rules of sound exegesis. Actually, honest and intelligent analysis of this great body of texts only serves to strengthen and confirm God's oft repeated claim that a saved person can never be lost.

The real issue remains: what will I do with the divinely dispensed knowledge of my security? What will *you* do with it? Will it predispose us to a life of sin or holiness? A life of spiritual sacrifice or selfish indulgence? Will we see our freedom as a license to sin or a liberty to serve?[5] Will we choose either licentiousness or legalism, or will this wondrous Grace on God's part inspire love and devotion on ours?

Of the many, many texts we might consider, for now, let's choose one – Ephesians 2:6. Having told us in verse five that, when we were doornail dead in the sphere of offenses, God made us alive with Christ ("by Grace [we] are saved"), God continues in verse six to say, "... and raised us up together, and seated us together in heavenly places in Christ Jesus." God goes on in verse 7 to give His reason for giving us dead people life, raising us up with Christ, and seating us in Heaven in our union with Christ. It is that, in eternity future, He might go on demonstrating the infinite wealth of His Grace by His kindness toward us in Christ Jesus. So, as always, here also our salvation is not based on our being given a second chance to do better than we did, but on who and what God is, and what He has accomplished by uniting us to Christ in His death, His resurrection, and His present and eternal position at God's right hand.

Seated! Seated! Seated in Heaven! Seated with Christ right next to the Father Himself! Forever! Does *this* sound as if we are on probation? Does it sound like Satan might do something, or we might do something to pull us from Heaven's throne, throw us out of Heaven itself, and return us to a lost, dead position on Earth, in the sphere of offenses and sins, and *apart* from Christ?!

How evil the thinking that man or devil can undo what God has done in His great wisdom and power!

Five times in Hebrews and eight times total in Scripture, Christ is said to be seated in Heaven. Unlike the priests on Earth who never sat because their work was never finished, Christ is a *seated* High Priest. For earthly priests there were always more sacrifices to offer... thousands more... millions more. His priestly work is finished; His once-for-all offering of Himself as a full and complete atonement for our sins was accepted by God the Father for time and eternity. He lives forever, and so never needs to be replaced. His substitutionary death avails for us forever, and so, *never* needs to be repeated.

There were thousands of priests in Israel at any given time. They are mentioned in Hebrews in contrast to the *ONE* priest for the Body of Christ. That's right... *ONE!* There has never been but one priest for Christians and there never will be. There is no need for priest or priestess. "There is one God and one Mediator between God and men, Himself man, Christ Jesus."[6] Our great "go-between" has gone between; He went between on Calvary's cross, forsaken by God and man. Both God the Son and God the Spirit are said to intercede in Heaven for believers, but they intercede, not as active priests, but on the basis of Christ's finished work on the cross.[7] "Finished," He shouted in triumph on the cross.[8] "Unfinished" shouts religion today, including "Christian" religions.

All denominations, ancient or modern, large or small, should accept God's invitation to study the Epistle to the Hebrews. Find a priest in Hebrews other than our Great High Priest. You won't. It can't be done. There *is* no other priest... and none is needed![9]

Religious man, even Christian religious man, will always resist the Holy Spirit and His message of uncompromised Grace. The poet said,

> "Jesus paid it all;
> all to Him I owe.
> Sin had left a crimson stain;
> He washed it white as snow."[10]
> — Mrs. J.M. Hall

Religion always denies that Christ paid it all on Calvary. Religion is man's defense against God's righteousness. It is innate to religion to deny that God does all the saving, that salvation is *all* of Grace. Man, left to himself, will always attempt to add his own merit to God's Grace. If you add arsenic to the baby's bottle, you no longer have milk; you have poison. Instead of giving life, it will bring death. Forget our sins for the moment. God says of our *righteous* acts that they are "filthy rags."[11] If you and I can't stand before God in Heaven's courtroom, dressed in the filthy rags of our own imagined goodness, would more filthy rags help? God tells us over and over that human righteousness is totally unacceptable to

Him. That is *WHY* Christ had to die! Human righteousness being an offense to an infinitely Holy God, a different type of righteousness must be found.

Walter Wilson, M.D., the physician turned author and radio Bible teacher, said, "Man cannot possibly stand before the bar of Heaven clad in his own righteousness. Nor can man *fail* to stand before the bar of Heaven dressed in the righteousness of God!" God *CANNOT* accept human righteousness. If He could, Christ need not have died.[12] God can *ONLY* accept His own righteousness, provided at Calvary, and offered free to any sinner who will only believe.

When the Philippian jailor asked, "What must I do to be saved?" Paul answered, "Believe on the Lord Jesus Christ and you shall be saved."[13] There aren't 7 things to do, or 4, or even two... just one! The sinner is to "believe on," to trust in Christ, and God will surely save. There are no "ifs, ands, or buts," no conditions, no strings attached, no surprises. We believe... God saves! It is a simple statement of fact.[14] We sinners perform the action of the verb "to believe," and God performs the action of the verb "to save." Notice the certainty of it all. Paul didn't say, "Believe and you *might* be saved," but believe and you *SHALL* be saved. If we do the only thing that God requires, God will do ALL the saving. God has never once failed to grant salvation, full and free, in response to faith. *NEVER*! And He never will fail! If we don't have the assurance that God grants in His Word, we doubt His integrity. God isn't bargaining with men for His pound of flesh – man's merit. God is rescuing ruined, rebellious, wretched, powerless sinners who have no merit. Nothing less than the death of Christ can get you into Heaven; nothing more than that is needed!

Religion has replaced God's Word with man's traditions, and this is our problem. Instead of subjecting human viewpoint to the scrutiny of Scripture, man does just the opposite; he sits in judgment on God's Word, using his own groupthink as the touchstone of truth and error. What supreme arrogance! Pipsqueak man deciding what the infinite Creator must say and do.

The fulness *and* freeness of salvation is the classic point in view. Religious man – and even atheists are religious – recognizes his debt to God, but insists that he can pay it off himself. Man offering God his merit, performance, and production in return for a cancelled debt is the common thread that runs through every religion. As startling as it may seem, man is incapable of thinking otherwise! When man thinks of salvation, he automatically thinks of a set of scales where human good is weighed against human evil. God thinks of a cross where man's total debt is paid in full by Another. Humans *would* not and *could* not have invented the cross, where God does all the giving and you and I do only all the receiving.

We cannot invite God into our living room and bargain with Him. We must meet Him at His cross, where there is *NO* bargaining, where there is nothing to bargain – where death, the wages of sin, has already been paid and no room is left for scales.

This is why it is such an abomination when well-meaning people couch salvation in terms of their "doing." "I gave my heart to Jesus." "I surrendered my life to God." "I made a commitment." "I asked Jesus into my heart." "I turned my life over to Christ."

Can you imagine a U.S. President, a Senator, Governor, football hero, beauty queen, or movie star saying, "I knelt as a criminal before a cruel and criminal cross and trusted the Savior for my salvation," or "I went to Calvary, hat-in-hand and Christ saved me," or "I brought only my sins to Christ at Calvary; He brought the righteousness of God as a gift to me"? Wouldn't you think that every one of us ruined, wretched, lost, rebellious sinners would mention the cross, and the Christ of the cross when we testify? Wouldn't you think that we Christians would leap at every chance to tell the world that we were saved at the foot of the cross, where Christ did *ALL* the giving while we did only *ALL* the receiving. God doesn't save Presidents, millionaires, football heroes, beauty queens, ladies and gentlemen; He saves sinners! Okay?

What is God saying about you when He says that *He* seated *you* at His own right hand – in Christ, a blessing never granted to the elect angels, the saved who lived before He formed the Body of Christ, or those who will be saved after our translation? He is saying that, spiritually, you are a finished package – complete in Christ.[15] Your body will catch up to your spirit at the Rapture. Until then, you are a saved person living in a unsaved body; a new creation being living in the old creation.

Ought we not to live, in dependence upon God, of course, like new creatures? Isn't that *why* we're new creatures? Isn't that *why* we were created anew?

A Jehovah Witness once asked me rhetorically, "You don't think that Paul was ever *completely* saved, do you?" Obviously, no one has ever been incompletely pregnant, dead, or lost. We are either "condemned" or "not condemned" in Scripture.[16] We have everlasting life or we are perishing.[17] We are saved or we are lost. We are seated with Christ or NOT seated with Him. Which are you? There is no third option. There is no middle ground.

"Seated in Heaven!" That has a ring of finality about it. God meant it to! Does that ring resonate with you?

CHAPTER EIGHTEEN NOTES

1. Hebrews 7:25; John 15:24; John 10:28-29
2. Romans 8:38-39
3. Philippians 1:6
4. Hebrews 5:9
5. Galatians 5:13
6. I Timothy 2:5
7. Romans 8:26,34
8. John 19:30
9. Romans 8:34; Ephesians 1:20; Colossians 3:1; Hebrews 1:3,13; 8:1; 10:12
10. Hymn, "Jesus Paid It All" by Mrs. H.M. Hall
11. Isaiah 64:6
12. Galatians 2:21
13. Acts 16:30-31
14. John 3:18,36
15. Colossians 2:9-10
16. John 3:18
17. John 3:16

CHAPTER NINETEEN

GOD WORKS IN YOU

Philippians 2:13 says, "For it is God who works in you both to will and to do of His good pleasure." Isn't this exciting? God Himself, the Creator of this vast and mind-boggling Universe, takes time for, and gives priority to, working in every believer – in you and in me. What an encouragement this has been to me when I have been mildly discouraged or even greatly depressed. God never gives up! In spite of my eccentricities, idiosyncracies, faults, weaknesses, stupidities, and yes, even my *sins,* God has been there for me, working *in* me, and always and forever *will* be!

I can hear someone saying, "Hey Duke, don't forget the rule of *context*!" Right. It has been noted that, "A text without a context is a pretext." So let's look. The preceding verse tells the Philippians to "work out your own salvation with fear and trembling." This verse, verse 12, has troubled millions. The troubling spot is the word "salvation." It comes from the Greek verb "sozo," meaning "to deliver, to save." Sometimes context requires that we understand it as a reference to our deliverance from condemnation, past, present, and future. If you haven't been delivered from any possibility of *ever* standing condemned before God, you haven't been saved at all. If you haven't been saved from any possibility of ever being cast into the Lake of Fire, you are unsaved. Remember, Christ didn't die to be your probation officer, but to be your Savior. Christ, in Scripture, not only saves from past, present, and future sins (plural), but saves us from sin (singular), the *sin nature* that we brought with us from Adam's loins; not only from what we do, but from who we were without Him.[1] The person we were in sin and under condemnation no longer exists, but died with Christ.[2]

But "salvation" in the Bible does not always refer to our receiving eternal life, escaping future condemnation, and passing out of death and into life.[3] Frequently, as in our text, Philippians 2:12, it refers to some other type of deliverance. In chapter one, Paul enlists the prayers of the Philippians "...that in nothing I shall be ashamed, but in all boldness, as always, now also Christ shall be magnified in my body whether by life or by death. For to me to live is Christ and to die gain."[4] Paul has always magnified Christ and requests the prayers of his friends that he will continue to do so right up to, and including the moment of death. The gain here is not Heaven, though that is certainly gain for the believer; the gain is magnifying Christ in the hour of his execution. In First Corinthians 9: 24-27, Paul expresses his determination to run the race of life and ministry all the way to final victory and not to be disqualified. He races because he *is* saved, not to *become* saved as bubblegum "theologians" would spin the passage!

The believers in Philippi are running a race too, and doing well according to the first half of verse 12, but they need the same deliverance Paul needs – deliverance from disqualification, from being put to shame, from failing to magnify Christ in their future as they had magnified Him in their past. This is the deliverance they are to "work out." Someone tell the Body of Christ that this is not salvation from condemnation, it's salvation from failure!

When you were saved, God put a spiritual workshop in your head! Big things can, and should, be accomplished in that shop. *God's* shop in *your* head is what Christian life and ministry is all about. There life takes place. How much God has been able to accomplish in and through you since the moment of your salvation has depended on your attitudes and action. You have to show up every morning to be worked on, and in, and through. What happens daily in your head determines what is accomplished daily in your life and ministry. Life's meaning, purpose, direction, progress, and final result is fashioned there. God wants to work with you daily to advance the ongoing miracle of your new life that began when you trusted Christ alone for your eternal salvation. Our greatest needs are met when God is able to move freely in our lives. God actively functioning in you is His number one priority regarding you, and needs to be your number one priority regarding Him.

Our text, verse thirteen, names only two things that God works in us, but these two things encapsulate the entire rhyme and reason for our existence. First, God works in us "to will... of His good pleasure." The verb "to will" here is used in Scripture to signify "to desire, to purpose, to plan." He also works in us to "do" His good pleasure!

It all starts with desire. Christ said, "...*I delight* to do Thy will, O my God."[5] If delighting in the Father's will is the norm for our Lord, it is the norm for us, too. One of the things your new birth brought with it is a desire to please God. That new desire may have begun in you as a blaze, or perhaps as just a little spark. In my own case, it began as a blaze that dwindled to a spark. The good news is that God is in the business of making sparks into flames, and flames into greater and greater flames. I pray several times a day this sentence prayer, "Dear Lord, please fan the flame of love for You until it consumes me." It doesn't need to always take the same form or use the same words; prayer that becomes vain repetition is dead and useless. It is not really prayer at all. While the words may vary, the essential request is the same, "Lord, help me to know You better, love You more, and serve You always."

Pray your own prayers. Find your own words. Prayers don't have to be long, but they need to be frequent. A sentence that comes from the heart will accomplish more than any Niagara of words that we *say*, but don't *pray*. Prayer isn't meant to twist the arm of a reluctant God; but heartfelt prayer can bring His answer and drive our lives in the right direction.

Do you desire to please God? If not, pray until you do, and then continue to pray for more and more desire. Live and die praying for this God-given desire. May God's will actually become our will. Nothing else really matters, because "Only Christ Matters!"

The phrase, "to will" not only can mean "to desire," but "to purpose." For the Christian, pleasing God (what life is all about!) must not stop with desire. Desire must become "purpose." Pleasing

God needs to become my reason for living, my direction, my goal, really, what I'm all about. My desire must not degenerate into wishful thinking. Wishful thinking is not faith. "Faith comes by...the Word of God."[6] A Christ-driven life is never just a dream. Dreams have a tendency to evaporate.

Lives have plans. That brings us to the third Scriptural meaning of the Greek word rendered "will" in our English versions of the Bible. God desires; God purposes; God plans, and so must we. Once I desire God's "good pleasure," once I determine to do what pleases Him for my lifetime, I must plan to actually carry out my desired purpose.

God delights in working in us! When we delight in *having* him work in us, things happen. Leonard Heroo said, "If you want to be spiritual, start making overtures to spirituality." This requires a plan of action. Simple things often make great plans! The Twelve "[gave] themselves to prayer and the ministry of the Word."[7] Simple, right?! If I devote myself to prayer and the ministry of the Word, I must plan the necessary steps to do this. I must budget my time and money so that I can put Christ first – really first – in my life, without sacrificing my God-given responsibilities to my family, for instance.

The serious Christian life is a life of choices. When one chooses to be wholly His in practice as well as in position, all subsequent decisions become easier.

The decision to desire, purpose, plan, and do the will of God is the most difficult decision the believer can make. It would be utterly impossible to carry through, but for the fact that "God works" in us to accomplish these four things: to desire, to determine, to design, and to do. "God works." The verb literally means "to energize," or more simply "energizes." "God energizes" in us. As you can see, it is the word for operational power. God is operating within us.

You cannot pray regularly, continuously, with a sense of urgency without your mindset changing and your attitude improving. Prayer from the very heart of you will cement your will and arouse your creativity. If prayer brings divine enablement in the first three, the fourth will follow supernaturally.

Do you really want to hotly pursue the things that are well-pleasing to your Creator and Savior, or just to eke out a spiritually mediocre existence in your little cocoon, your comfort zone, unthreatened by the high cost of following Christ?

Most believers choose the latter, and spend life defending their choice. What have *you* chosen?

We believers will spend the eternal future, the never-ending tomorrow, free of sin and doing always "those things that please Him." This earthly life, this skinny little slice of time, affords us an unique opportunity to serve Him at high cost to ourselves. This is a challenge that will never be available again. If you and I were in Heaven right now enjoying the greatest, most unimaginable comfort zone, and an angel came to us and told us that God wanted volunteers to visit a planet for 70 years (give or take a few) where we would glorify Him and serve man, in Satan's world system, in an evil age, in difficult circumstances, among hostile enemies and ungrateful friends, surrounded by fears and indwelt by conflict, what would you say? What would I?

God's good pleasure. This is what we were created for. We exist for Him, not He for us. Much of today's teaching, much of our evangelism, encourages people to think that God exists for us, that any God worthy of the name would jump at the chance to be an automaton, our Heavenly candy machine, the great bell-hop in the sky. This "big rock candy mountain" view of things cheapens God. It robs Him of His glory, marginalizes His majesty, reduces Him to the pocket-sized gods of pagan society.

But God works in you! If you will let Him!

CHAPTER NINETEEN NOTES

1. I Corinthians 15:3; Romans 6:10
2. Romans 6:2; 7:17,20; Galatians 2:20
3. John 5:24
4. Philippians 1:20-21
5. Hebrews 10:7
6. Romans 10:17
7. Acts 6:4

CHAPTER TWENTY

NEW POWER FOR A NEW LIFE

~

Colossians 3:4 says, "When Christ, our life, shall appear, then shall you also appear with Him in glory."

The world asks four questions: Who am I? Where did I come from? Why am I here? Where am I going? The answers are in God's Book, and have been there for 2,000 years, but the world eagerly scraps intellect in favor of emotion when it comes to the things that really matter. So does a worldly church.

Who am I? "A leather bag filled with chemicals," says the humanist, borrowing from Marxism as humanists do with nearly all of their major tenets. "An accident of time and chance," say pseudo-scientists, abandoning legitimate science in favor of the ancient Babylonian religious myth of macro evolution. Anthony Flew is hardly the only evolutionary apologist to abandon random chance for an intelligent Creator. He made the gigantic leap from atheism to theism, because he could not, in good conscience, credit mindless time and chance with producing the mind-boggling complexities of the DNA chain.

Christ is the believer's life – every believer's. This statement is clear and unequivocal. It is also bombastic! Christ is our life! Not Christ plus my church, be it Protestant, Catholic, Orthodox, or otherwise! Not Christ plus my peers, my heroes, my superiors! Not Christ plus Mary! Christ is the only life that flows through my spiritual veins. "In Him dwells all the fullness of the Godhead bodily."[1] No wonder the next verse tells us "And [we] are, in Him, complete."[2] This statement – that Christ is our life – is not just poetry, nor just sentiment, but theology, science, and fact. It will stand proven empirically in eternity future as it stands proven Scripturally in present time.

The 20th verse of chapter two says, "Assuming then you died with Christ away from the rudimentary principles of the world, why *as if alive in the world* do you subject yourselves to ordinances?"[3] The first verse of chapter three begins, "Assuming then you were raised with Christ...."[4] The believer, you and I who have died with Christ, have been raised with Christ, and we are asked by God and Paul, "...why do you subject yourselves to ordinances, as if alive in the world?" Why are we trying to live new life under old rules, in the power of the old life? Christ was conceived, born, raised under Law, lived and died under Law, but rose out of Law into resurrection life, and we died and rose with Him.

Have you ever heard a sermon about *your* resurrection life? Has anyone ever told you that you have resurrection life *NOW – this side of Heaven*? "If anyone is in Christ there is a new creation: the old things passed away; Look! All things have become new."[5] You don't have to wait until you get to Heaven to enjoy resurrection life. You are a new creation being already, even though you still live in the old creation. Your "forever life" is flowing through your spiritual veins *RIGHT NOW*! Don't expect the world to recognize you; your old creation body looks the same as it did when you were unsaved. You are a saved person living in an unsaved body![6] Don't expect your loved ones, relatives and friends, to understand you, since I Corinthians 2:15 says that they *CANNOT*. Love them, pray for them, serve them (love serves), and witness to them, but don't require them to figure you out. The natural person *will* not because he *can* not.

But *you* need to know who *you* are! You are in Christ. Union with Christ is the least appreciated Grace doctrine – and the most important! When you did the only thing a person can do without doing anything – you trusted in what Another had done – you died and rose with Him!

You died to the world. Paul tells us in Galatians 6:14, "But may it not be for me to boast except in the cross of our Lord Jesus

Christ; through whom the world has been crucified to me, *and I to the world."*

You died to your sinful nature, and to the person you were previously – in sin and under condemnation. It is a thing of the past.[7]

You died to Law; it can no longer condemn you.[8]

You died to religion, with its "touch not, taste not, handle not" – its rituals, rites, and priesthood.[9] You have only one Priest, one Mediator, who is seated with God in Heaven, having completed His priestly work.[10]

You are a completely new "you," still plagued with some of your old problems. A part of the future confined to the present, but just for awhile. You are one person with two natures, and the nature you feed will thrive, will dominate! You have the power to disgrace your Lord – or to honor Him. You must choose. God *will not* force the choice on you, and Satan would if he could, but he can't.

Salvation is an event; practical sanctification is a process. Salvation is instantaneous, complete, and eternal; daily holiness is just that – daily. Sanctification, or holiness, is simply "set-apart-ness;" it is not mystical, magical, spookiness. There is no such thing as good spookiness. Religion is full of spooky people who are venerated by people who have no desire to be spooky themselves. God is not the author of spookiness, but the author of holiness – separation. When you were saved, God "saint-ified" you; He set you apart from a lost race. Now He calls you to saint-ify yourself, to set yourself apart from bondage, enslavement to your sinful, Adamic nature. "Choose you this day whom you will serve."[11]

One of the worst traps we can fall into is that of accepting the heresy of "virtual sinless perfection." Most believers escape the heresy of "absolute sinless perfection" – or a "second definite work of Grace," an experience where one's sinful nature is "removed, root and branch." This is sometimes called "perfect love," or "entire sanctification," or "perfect holiness." The same 6th chapter of Romans that says we are to "consider [ourselves] to be actually dead to sin,"[12] goes on to say, "therefore stop letting sin reign in your mortal body." Here it is obvious that the same Romans who were dead as a doornail to sin were still being mastered by it. Our death to sin is *positional*, not *experiential*. To know this is to have the key to

Romans six, and the key to Christian life and victory. We are dead to sin in Heaven's courtroom. But in our daily lives we are very much alive to it. Our perfect position before God makes possible victory over sin in our experience.

While most believers know, at least intuitively, that the struggle between our two natures is a lifelong series of battles, they are often taught that they have but one nature – the new nature. Recently, I heard a "one nature preacher" loudly and angrily condemning the doctrine of the two natures of the believer as a "damnable heresy." "When you accepted Christ," he said, "your old nature just got up and walked away." He then spent 40 minutes preaching against sin in the believer's life. This type of contradiction pervades our evangelicalism today. It produces confusion in the minds of believers and frustration in their lives.

Scripture is clear; "...the flesh passionately desires against the spirit, and the spirit against the flesh; and these things are opposed to one another, that you should not do whatever you may wish."[13]

The *bad* news is that the flesh has passionate cravings that are incredibly powerful. The *good* news is that the spirit has passionate cravings that are incredibly powerful. The *best* news is that, if we "walk by means of the spirit, [we] will in no wise fulfill the desire of the flesh."[14]

If you've been saved for even a little while, you know something of the awesome power of the flesh. If you've been saved for some length of time, you know that the flesh refuses to be your servant or even your partner! The flesh insists on being your king, on ruling over your mortal body.[15] This is why you and I cannot say "yes" to a little bit of sin. The flesh is like a camel that is not content to get only its nose in your tent. The whole camel will surely follow its nose! You cannot say "yes" to a little sin without saying "yes" to a lot! Sin will never serve you. It will never partner with you. It will insist on reigning in your mortal body till death do you part. A man cannot serve two masters, Christ taught, he will love one and hate the other. Christ reigns in you or sin reigns. Sin will not share the throne with Christ, and Christ will not share the throne with sin.

Your new nature is more powerful than your old nature, simply because its source of supply is God the Father, God the Son, God the Spirit, and the dynamic of God's Word! All your old nature has to rely on is Satan and Satan's world – no match for God. Not even close! Sadly, most believers who recognize the Scriptural teaching that each of us has two natures, know only the power of one – the wrong one! Sadly, too, that most believers don't realize that we are "citizens of Heaven on loan to Planet Earth," nor that God has *completely equipped us* for this very thing, and only for this very thing! God has perfectly equipped us to live life on a mission, according to plan. Our very purpose is "to glorify God and enjoy Him forever,"[16] and not to be healthy, wealthy, and happy. There is nothing intrinsically wrong with health, wealth, or happiness, but they must not take over from an urgent sense of mission, nor from a consuming devotion to Christ.

Colossians tells us that we are not "alive in the world." Our life is not the old life that we had when we were "of the world." We still live "in the world," but our life is Heaven life, not Earth life. It is the same life that flows through the "veins" of the people who are in Heaven right now, and the same life that will flow through your spiritual veins for eternity future!

"He that believes *has* [lit. "and holds"] eternal life."[17] Our life is already eternal in quantity *because* it is eternal in quality! It is "forever life" because it is "divine life." Our Lord said, "that which has been born of the Spirit [capital "S"] is spirit [small "s"]"![18] The phrase "born again" has suffered more from its friends than its enemies, but it is infinitely more than just words. You and I, at the exact moment that we trusted Christ, were "born of God." Conceived, gestated, and born – all in less than a second of time! How can you and I live any longer in the energy of the flesh, and by the fleshly rules, "carnal ordinances" imposed on "once-born" people? We are pilgrims! We must pass through Vanity Fair, but we're equipped to live above it – and designed to live beyond it!

CHAPTER TWENTY NOTES

1. Colossians 2:9
2. Colossians 2:10
3. Colossians 2:20
4. Colossians 3:1
5. II Corinthians 5:17
6. Romans 8:22,23
7. Romans 6:11; Romans 6:2,3
8. Romans 7:4
9. Colossians 2:20-21
10. I Timothy 2:5; Hebrews 1:3; 4:14-16
11. Joshua 24:15
12. Romans 6:11-12
13. Galatians 5:17
14. Galatians 5:16
15. Romans 6:12
16. Westminster Shorter Catechism
17. John 6:47
18. John 3:6

CHAPTER TWENTY-ONE

UNLOCKING TIME

～

There are keys to understanding Scripture. One is the *attitude* you bring with you to your study of the Word. You may come to the Bible believing that it is true and having your initial faith confirmed consistently, or you may approach the Bible predisposed to reject it and find a never-ending series of unanswered questions to deepen your doubts.

In the 1950's, there were two evangelists whose ministries promised to change history. Chuck Templeton chose doubt of the Word as his foundation for life and ministry. Unbelief brought him to a life of discouragement, depression, and finally despair. Suicidal tendencies wrought havoc with his "faith." Billy Graham chose to take God at His Word. In his preaching, he constantly repeated, "The Bible says..."; "The Scriptures declare..."; "The Word of God teaches..."; "Christ said...." Graham's faith grew as God's Word proved true thousands of times, and his audiences found their own faith growing stronger in response to the reliable statements of this unique Book.

The key of *attitude* is not "blind faith." It is adopting the position that the Bible is what it claims to be, seems to be, and proves to be to honest hearts.

Another key is *accuracy* – making sure that you are reading exactly what is written. Men frequently misquote the Bible. For instance, some say, "Money is the root of all evil," but Christ did not say that. He said "The *LOVE* of money is the root of all [manner] of evil."[1]

Still another key is *context*. Matthew 24:13 says, "He that endures to the end shall be saved." Millions have made shipwreck of their faith by imposing a meaning on this statement that violates the rule of context. They have wrongly assumed that "the end" in this verse refers to the end of one's life. It doesn't! The phrase "the end," which appears four times in this passage, refers to the end of the future Great Tribulation. Believers, both Jew and Gentile, who survive this worst nightmare in human history, will be saved, or delivered. The salvation, or deliverance, in view is not our salvation from sin and condemnation, from sin's penalty of being lost forever, but deliverance from a time of unprecedented pressure and unimaginable horror when God pours out His wrath on a generation of totally rebellious humans who have willfully chosen Satan over Christ.

Yet another key is *language* itself. God wrote the "Old Testament" largely in Hebrew with a small portion in Aramaic. The "New Testament" He wrote in Greek. Our English versions, and those in other languages, are not Bibles in the strict sense, but are translations of the one Bible that God "breathed."[2] God wrote only one Bible, and He wrote it in Hebrew, Aramaic, and Greek. God never wrote a word in English!

When one reads an English translation of the New Testament, he finds the word "servant" many times. Unfortunately, translators have used this one English word to represent a wide variety of Greek words with different meanings such as "helper, domestic, hired hand, civil servant, religious attendant, and slave." God purposely chose different Greek words to communicate His meaning precisely. Much is lost to our understanding when God's accuracy is sacrificed on the altar of man's carelessness, or even stubbornness. Also, when man renders the Greek word for Passover – a divinely ordained Jewish feast – by the word "Easter" which signifies a pagan celebration, God's right to choose His own words with care is violated.

Whenever any message longer than a "STOP" sign is moved from one language to another, some loss in meaning is unavoidable. Some Greek words, for instance, have no corresponding English word to accurately convey the richness of their meanings.

Then, too, it sometimes requires more words to communicate to the English reader what a few words in Greek do for the reader in Greek.[3] Our English versions say, "For by Grace you are saved," but there are two forms of the verb "to be" here. "You are" is in the present tense, with linear or ongoing action. "Saved" is in the perfect tense, which refers to an action completed in time past with present, usually permanent, results. To do God's Word, and our understanding, justice, we would have to render it, "For by unmerited favor you continue [present tense] having been completely saved in time past, with the result that you are still completely saved" (perfect tense).

We can see at a glance how full this statement is in the Greek in which God wrote it, and how much it has lost in most English translations. Then the periphrasis goes on to say, "And this [salvation] not of yourselves; it is God's gift: not of works, that not anyone might boast." Taken as God wrote it, it declares in unmistakable terms the self-evident truth that all the saved are secure forever and can never, ever be lost. Christ is our Savior, not our probation officer! Christ's death in Scripture is a "once-for-ever" death, making our salvation a "once-for-ever" salvation. Those passages that seem to teach that a saved person can be lost prove on examination not to teach that at all. Some of them, studied in context and with due regard for the real meaning of their words, actually teach the opposite of the false claims they are called on to support – they actually teach the *eternal security* of the saved.

Salvation in Scripture is never a second chance, an opportunity to do better, or a clean page to write on. It is only that in religion, never in God's Word. The truth is that man cannot possibly stand before an absolutely Holy God dressed in his own righteousness, nor can he fail to stand before God dressed in the righteousness of God, given as a free gift to all that believe. A lifetime of my own personal righteousness can not erase the smallest of my sins, let alone give me a new and perfect right standing before a God so Holy that He must condemn all sin – every sin. If my righteous acts are but "filthy rags"[4] in God's sight, then can a thousand lifetimes make me one ounce less lost? A million lifetimes, each one of which outdid Mother Theresa's, would not move me one inch closer to salvation.

Our problem is not that we do not have *enough* righteousness, but that *WE DO NOT HAVE ANY AT ALL!*

This made it necessary for God to become a man and to die on a cross for hopeless and helpless sinners! The bad news is that nothing less than the death of Christ on His cross can get us into Heaven; the good news is that nothing more than that is needed! Leonard Heroo asked, "How do I know that I am a great sinner?" He then answered, "Because it took almighty God Himself to die in my place!" I may, and I should, show my appreciation to God for being my Savior by my good works, but a lifetime of good works can add nothing to the crosswork of God's Son. God the Son, on Calvary, completely satisfied the righteous demands of God the Father. God satisfied God! Religion denies this; God's Word affirms it. Which side do *you* come down on, God's or religion's? Whom do you trust, God or man?

Still another key to understanding the Bible lies in *recognizing figures of speech.* Man's languages are fraught with figures of speech, and God employed man's languages – Hebrew, Aramaic, and Greek to communicate His Word. Literal speech is *never* to be taken figuratively. Figurative speech is *never* to be taken literally. Great harm occurs when this rule is violated.

I read recently of a man who gouged out his right eye because he had "eyes full of adultery, and that cannot cease from sin."[5] Didn't Christ say to pluck out your eye if it offends you? Of course He did, but He was speaking figuratively – stressing the awfulness of our sin nature with its consequent sins. If he meant "pluck out your eye" literally, most of us would have run out of eyes in short order. Guide dogs would have overrun the world by now.

Christ is spoken of in the Bible as a rock, a lamb, a lion, a shepherd, a door, bread, a sower, a vine; but all these are figures of speech. He said, "He that eats my flesh and drinks my blood, has life eternal...."[6] That this also is figurative is plain from what He had just said seconds before, "I am the bread of life; he that COMES to me shall never hunger,"[7] (coming is "eating"), "And he that BELIEVES on me shall never thirst" (believing is "drinking"). A key to this entire chapter is in verse 63, "It is the Spirit who makes alive; the flesh profits nothing; *the words that I speak to you are spirit and life.*" The same Bible which says to us, "That rock was Christ,"[8] which can ONLY mean, "That rock *represented* Christ," also quotes Christ saying, "This is my body," which can ONLY mean, "This represents my body." Many foolish myths arise when men mistake figurative for literal, and literal for figurative. You had better "eat" Christ spiritually, (come to Him in faith), or you will not "eat" Him at all!

Yet another key to unlocking God's Word is provided when we *observe who is being addressed.* I don't write the same letter to the gas company that I write to my wife. Neither do you. We have different messages for different people, and so does God. Say a woman has two daughters – one sixteen and one six. She leaves a note on the refrigerator for each. To the teen, she says, "Take the van to the gas station and fill it up, then have it washed." To the first grader she says, "Pick up your toys, straighten up your room, and mind your sister." Imagine what could happen if they took each other's notes by mistake, and the little sister tried to drive the van to the gas station!

Every year, millions of Christians read, "If two of you should agree on Earth concerning anything they shall ask, it shall be done for them by my Father who is in Heaven. For where two or three are gathered together in my Name, there am I in the midst of them."[9] They apply this temporary provision, addressed to the Twelve, to themselves. They find someone to agree with them, pray together, and nothing happens. The Twelve were practicing Jews; they were still going to the temple, circumcising their children, offering animal sacrifices, and zealously observing the Law thirty years after Pentecost. At the time Christ made this promise, they were not yet indwelt by the Holy Spirit. YOU ARE! God resides in you, and you don't need two or three to have Christ present. If you are otherwise alone, Christ is with you. If your prayer is according to God's revealed will in Scripture, God will do what you ask! If your prayer is not aligned with God's will, lots of luck, my friend!

In the Bible, God speaks to many individuals and groups. Every promise in the book is *NOT* mine! Nor every warning! God speaks to angels – both elect and fallen, to Satan, to humans – saved and lost, to Israel, the Gentiles, the Body of Christ, the animal creation, the inanimate creation, and even to demons. Somewhere in this litany, you'll find you. God even has differing instructions for the same individual or group in one lifetime. Adam was to stay in the Garden and be its landscaper, but he sinned and was told to get out and stay out. Israel was to occupy the promised land and then God dispersed them throughout the nations of the world – and will yet regather them to their land! Peter was told to keep kosher and then *not* to keep kosher. The Twelve were commanded to go to all the world, and then to confine their ministry to Israel.

An often neglected key is *grammar*. The case of a noun, for instance, or the tense of a verb is just as much a part of God's Word as the noun or verb itself. If God says you died with Christ, don't ask him to crucify you or try to crucify yourself. If God says it's already done, it's done! If God says, "Having forgiven you ALL trespasses," believe Him and thank Him. But don't ask Him to do it again. Doing that is doubting God, and remember, "Without faith, it is impossible to please Him."[10] We should *never* insult Him with doubt.

Many English translations quote our Lord as saying, "Whatever you shall bind on Earth shall be bound in Heaven; and whatever you shall loose on Earth shall be loosed in Heaven."[11] A number of churches have assumed the prerogative of forgiving or refusing to forgive sins on the basis of this mistranslation. But Christ NEVER SAID THAT! He said, "Whatever you shall bind on Earth shall be WHAT HAS BEEN BOUND IN HEAVEN; and whatever you shall loose on Earth shall be WHAT HAS BEEN LOOSED IN HEAVEN"![12]

"What *HAS BEEN* bound," is a perfect passive participle – an action completed in time past with present day results. "What *HAS BEEN* loosed," is another perfect passive participle! Again, an action already completed whose *results remain*. Millions of professing Christians have been taught error through a disregard of the tense of the verbs "to bind" and "to loose."

If my church says one thing and God says another, whom shall I believe? Shall I believe my own groupthink, or God's Holy Word? Do I love some nameless, faceless monk from the dateless past more than I love my God and Savior Jesus Christ? That is *NOT* faith! That is *unbelief*! Now I must fish or cut bait! When God corrects man's error, shall I not come down on God's side?[13] And you?

In Galatians 2:20, Paul says literally, "I have been and remain crucified with Christ." He does *NOT* say, "I need to be," "I am in the process of becoming," "sometimes I am," "I am partly," or "I shall be someday." It is again in the perfect tense, and man has no right to change it – or to ignore it. To change the tense is to change God's Word! What God has written, He has written. No man has a right to alter it, and why would anyone in His right mind wish to? God chose the perfect tense to say what He wanted to say, because no other tense could do the job.

If you or I find a "difficult" passage, it will serve us well to *compare related passages*. This too, is a key to grasping the truth as God has communicated it. The miracle of the "feeding of the five thousand" appears in all four Gospels. Each parallel account supplies some information that the others do not. Also, consulting passages that relate to the same topic as the verse, or verses, in question, can bring necessary light and end needless confusion.

The entire book of Hebrews is a "Handbook of eternal security." To find a "problem verse" in chapter six or in chapter ten and ignore the great theme, the thrust, of the Book is to commit intellectual suicide as well as to rob God of His glory. To stumble over 6:1-8 while ignoring the key in verse 9, the actual language of verses 4-8, and the message of the book as a whole is abject foolishness. The people of verses 4-8 saw the Light of the world and rejected Him; had a "taste" of Christ's presence for a third of a century and said, "We don't want this man to reign over us." They had the testimony of the Holy Spirit from Acts 2 to Acts 28 and refused it, found the message of God's Word unpalatable, and were eye-witnesses of millennial age works of power and responded by re-crucifying their Savior. They are not once said to be saved, but the people of verse nine are!

The "willful sin" of Hebrews 10:26 is rejecting the Savior even after hearing a very clear statement concerning who and what He is, and *trampling* upon Him, *esteeming* His blood unclean – the covenant blood that sanctified, or set apart, the Nation Israel (making *NATIONAL* salvation possible), and *insulting* the Spirit of Grace. These people are never said to have been saved. Their response to the Gospel is clearly poles apart from saving faith.

All of the Bible is *FOR* us! One-thirteenth of the Bible is *TO* us and *ABOUT* us, but *ALL* of the Bible is *FOR* us...for our learning. We need to study it. Not to spend our short but valuable time on

Earth hunting down "proof texts" and twisting them to fit man's groupthink.

How much of our "faith" is simply what we want to believe, and how much is what *God* wants us to believe?

STUDY, MAN, STUDY!

CHAPTER TWENTY-ONE NOTES

1. I Timothy 6:10
2. II Timothy 2:15 (lit.)
3. Ephesians 2:8-9
4. Isaiah 64:6
5. II Peter 2:14
6. John 5:54
7. John 6:35
8. I Corinthians 10:4
9. Matthew 18:19
10. Hebrews 11:6
11. Matthew 18:18
12. Matthew 16:19
13. II Timothy 3:16

CHAPTER TWENTY-TWO

POWER IN PRAYER

There is power in prayer! Prayer can revolutionize your life, changing it dramatically. Serious prayer, coupled with serious Bible study, can take you from defeat to victory. Our Lord prayed and considered prayer important. He taught His followers to pray. For nineteen centuries His teaching on the subject of prayer has vastly improved the lives and ministries of millions. Our Apostle prayed, and reminded us never to give up on praying. If prayer was essential to the life and ministry of Christ, it must be essential to yours and mine. If Paul found prayer indispensable, it must be absolutely necessary to our success.

Prayer can be the difference between success and failure in life, but what is prayer? Unfortunately, most Christians view it as a means of controlling God – getting the Creator to do the creature's will. But prayer is intimacy. It is the normal reflection of a close relationship with God. To have God speak to us through His Word, the Bible, is our greatest privilege. To be invited to speak to Him is our highest honor. "What is man that you are mindful of him?"[1] Think of it! The one who created trillions of stars and calls them all by name has numbered the hairs of our heads and invites us into the most intimate fellowship with Himself. Almighty God wants to spend time with us, so time spent with Him is never time wasted.

It is tragic that Christendom has reduced life's greatest love affair to a matter of asking and receiving. Certainly that is an important part of our prayers, but when asking assumes precedence, prayer becomes impersonal and God becomes a "thing." Prayer should enable us to know God better, love Him more, and serve Him faithfully. It should enroll us in *His* program, not Him in *ours*. Christ prayed, "Not my will, but Yours be done."[2] We reverse that and seek to bend God to *our* will. Talking to God should submerge us forever in the plan of God, not cheapen Him by demanding that He immerse Himself in ours. Whenever I pray, I should do so because I appreciate who and what He is. When I finish, I should appreciate Him even more. Prayer should always deepen my affection for my Heavenly Father and reinforce my dedication to His cause.

What should I pray about? Pray for *people*. This big world may seem little different when you and I have passed through it, but we *can* change the little world in which we live; the world of parents, siblings, spouses, children, friends and even enemies. All of these are "neighbors" (near ones) – people we encounter on the pathway of life.

Pray about "*things*." God and Paul tell us in Philippians 4:4 to "Rejoice in the Lord always, and again I say, Rejoice" – literally, "Keep on rejoicing in the Lord always [present tense, linear action], and I repeat, keep on rejoicing." Depression is never the will of God for believers! Then, having set the stage for our prayer life, God and Paul tell us in verse six, "Stop being anxious about even one *thing*, but in every *thing* by prayer and asking with thanksgiving, let your requests be made known to God." The result of this kind of praying, set in the context of a life of rejoicing, is said to be God's peace made ours – a peace which goes way beyond our understanding (verse 7). This astounding level of peace, even in times of extreme adversity, "stands guard over our hearts and minds, [our attitude and thinking], in Christ Jesus."

Our prayers will not always be answered *our* way, but they will be answered *His* way, and hopefully you learned early in your Christian life that His way is best. Christ had supreme confidence that the Father's way is always best and rested in God's way, praying, "Your will, not mine" – your way, not mine – "be done."

"Rejoice...always" means simply, "find your happiness in Christ, and keep on finding it there."

You will never understand prayer this side of Heaven, any more than you will metabolism, but keep on eating anyway – and keep on praying. Praying, like eating, works!

Pray with *thanksgiving*. Take two different colored highlighters and go through Paul's Epistles. Highlight everything God changed when He saved you. Use one color to highlight the things that were true of you one second *before* you trusted Christ for your salvation that are no longer true of you *now*. Use the other to mark the *new* things that became true of you then and are still true of you now. Start every prayer by thanking God for one of these things and that He has changed them! You were without God, without Christ, without hope in the world and deservedly so. God changed that. You were "far off" but now you're nearby. Thank Him for it. As you read the whole Bible, and the Pauline Epistles in particular, you will find that you have great spiritual wealth. There are many things that became true of you the minute you trusted Christ's death as yours, for which you can breathe up a word of thanks.

Thanking God is a form of prayer – the best form. It is the proper place to start all prayer. Thankful people are seldom depressed. Being truly grateful is a most effective anti-depressant with no side effects! Besides, regular thanksgiving develops a grateful attitude and sets the tone of life and service. Grateful people are usually fun to be around. Ingrates are not. Complainers are not.

When should I pray and how long? Pray at all times. Prayers need not be long. "The Gentiles think they will be heard for their much speaking,"[3] said our Lord. Sentence prayers are great! Often, the heart of a matter can be expressed clearly in a few words. A prayer of only one sentence in length can be heard by God and answered as surely as a prayer of greater length. Our prayers don't have to fight their way to Heaven; God indwells us. Prayers don't have to pierce ceilings, penetrate clouds, or climb to the throne above. In my Pentecostal days, my beloved Pastor and friend, Joseph Payne, would say, "God is nearer than hands and feet; closer than the breath in our nostrils."

Which prayers get answered? True prayer agrees with the will of God. This is the only type of prayer that God has promised to answer. This is the real meaning of the phrase "in Jesus' name;" it is not a magic addendum to prayer or a "rabbit's foot." American ambassadors represent our Country. What they say and do overseas is what they have been sent to say and do. They speak to foreign officials in the name of the United States, but they don't end every conversation by saying, "in the name of the United States." To do that would be unnecessary, and quite frankly, foolish. It wouldn't give a "jet assist" to their words. And yet, in some quarters, men are considered heretics if they don't finish every prayer by saying, "in Jesus' name." A prayer that harmonizes with God's will as found in the Bible doesn't need to be tagged. A prayer that is contrary to God's Word won't be helped by tagging it. No one in Scripture ever closes a prayer by saying, "in Jesus' name." God never tells us to *say* "in Jesus' name," though we are always to *pray* in Jesus' name, meaning on Jesus' authority. Most prayers that close with the phrase, "in Jesus' name" are not prayed in Jesus' name, on Jesus' authority, nor could they be! This is why no one has ever moved a literal mountain by command. In the coming Day of the Lord, if Christ says to a believer, "I want this mountain moved," even "mustard seed faith" will respond to Christ's command and, in Jesus' name, on Jesus' authority, order the mountain to move and that mountain will move, friend! To actually *pray* in Jesus' name, as opposed to just *saying* "in Jesus' name" at the end of your prayer is to pray according to God's will revealed in God's Word. You may ask God to keep Grandma safe on her motorcycle, but you cannot ask it on the authority of Christ because *GOD HAS NOT TOLD YOU THAT IT IS HIS WILL* to keep Grandma safe! In spite of your praying and attaching your magic talisman to your prayer, Grandma may run her new Roadsmasher into a cow and wake up in a choirloft in Heaven.

Don't listen to some still, small voice you hear in your shower. It isn't God's voice! It may be Satan's voice, but it's probably yours! Since the Canon of Scripture closed, we have lived under a silent Heaven. God's Word claims to be complete and to be able to complete your understanding. Extra-Biblical revelation is a hallmark of the cults. Everything necessary to bring us to maturity is in the Bible, through which God offers to complete you for worship of, and service to Him. If that's not good enough, you have a problem. God was silent for the 400 years between the Old and New Testaments and He's been silent for 19 hundred years since. The next time God speaks will be in judgment! Marinate your head in Scripture and you won't go wrong!

Man makes many rules for prayer that God Himself hasn't made. Tradition frequently clouds truth. Prayer is conversation with our Heavenly Father. We should be reverent, but talk as we normally do. We should be ourselves in prayer; it is too precious to be degraded to a ritual, making us sound like someone we're not.

Most of us seem to know that we ought to pray. But, talking to God is a high privilege and should never become a chore. I ought to do it because I want to, never because I have to. Would any parent want a child to speak only because the child felt it must? Would a parent want a child's fellowship only in emergencies, or when the child wanted something? Too many parent/child relationships today have lost the intimacy of love and become strained and impersonal. A true relationship exists in an atmosphere of love, because the relationship creates the atmosphere. It's the same with our relationship to our Heavenly Father.

Many believers recognize that our lives should be characterized by prayer, but most believers seldom pray. This is because we have found prayer unsatisfying. Learning some basic, but rarely taught facts, can change all that in minutes. We can change a life of powerlessness for a lifetime of power in no time at all, but we need to get started now. My dad used to say, "Anything worth doing is worth doing well." Let's add, "Anything worth doing is worth starting now." To get started on a life of prayer, pray simple "sentence prayers." Examples include: "Lord, I thank You for saving me." "Lord, I thank You for this 24-hour slice of opportunity." "Lord, help me to honor You today in all that I do and say." "Lord, help our family to draw closer together." "Bless my enemies, O Lord, and help me to love them and bless them." "Please give me a heart that is quick to forgive, dear Savior." "Holy Spirit, please help me to understand and apply Your Word." "Give me an ever greater love for the Bible, Heavenly Father." "Father, I thank you for the indwelling Holy Spirit." "Thank you, Lord, for who and what You are." "Help me to depend on the power of Christ within." "Thank you for Calvary." "I love you, Lord; help me to love You more."

I would rather pray 100 sentence prayers a day than to go to an all-night prayer meeting (not to disparage all-night prayer meetings). Prayer should turn humdrum circumstances into the adventure of living. Remember, never quit praying! Never quitting anything we ought to be doing is the secret of success.

As a believer, you are a steward of your body, soul, and spirit, as well as your material possessions and your God-given responsibilities. You are a steward of your time and energy. Intelligent prayer can go a long way toward providing structure and discipline to every facet of your life. See temptation as a call to prayer. No believer need live in defeat. Determine that you will not accept defeat in your life and ministry. Even giving our thought life over to good things instead of best things can drain our energy and bleed away our time.

A young man in the roofing business who spent considerable time driving on Chicagoland expressways, most of it fuming about snarled traffic and careless and thoughtless drivers, attended our classes on "sentence praying." He decided to train himself to start praying sentences as soon as he sat in his truck every morning. Good habits, sometimes hard to form can be hard to break as well. Years ago, I began praying for each individual in my family as soon as my head hit the pillow. It has become so strong a habit that I cannot go to sleep now until I've prayed! Our friend, the roofer, let's call him Mac, soon had a fixed regimen of prayer. Each morning as he shuts the door of his truck, and inserts the ignition key, he begins to talk to God – informally, conversationally. No formal addresses. God is his Father and Mac talks to Him as a son. What once were countless hours of frustration, anxiety, disappointment and anger, now are eagerly anticipated times of pleasant fellowship with God.

Prayer keeps the believer's mind and affections fixed on "things above" and not on "things on Earth." True prayer does not interfere with safe driving, fulfilling responsibilities, or grasping opportunities. Sometimes in hectic rush-hour traffic, my sentence prayers become phrases only – even single words. I often pray "Things above, Lord," or just "things." God knows what I mean. Sometimes in the rat race of drivers changing lanes and jockeying for position, my prayer can be one word – "Father." God says "...think on these things,"[4] which I often reduce to "these things, Lord." God hears it as "Dear Heavenly Father, please help me to concentrate on the things that are spiritually profitable." At other times, sentences become paragraphs.

We who have children and grandchildren are to teach them by word and by example. Children soon learn from an example of prayerlessness that prayer is not important. That pathetic example may shape a young mind for life! If you regularly rattle off some words at the dinner table like, "Now we thank Thee for our food. Please bless it to the nourishment of our bodies," your children will soon learn to ignore it – even not to hear it at all, or, worse yet, to repeat it for a lifetime as mechanically as they heard you do! It is a great blessing for children to hear parents and/or grandparents pray earnest, joyous, heartfelt prayers, especially when the prayers are shaped by the Word of God, rightly divided, and kept short and sweet!

Prayerful believers who voraciously devour God's Word daily and rightly divide it are a great influence "at home and abroad." Be one...and do it!

CHAPTER TWENTY-TWO NOTES

1. Psalm 8:4; Hebrews 2:6
2. Luke 22:42
3. Matthew 6:7
4. Philippians 4:8

CHAPTER TWENTY-THREE

THE MYSTERY

~

You have probably noticed in your study of the Word that the early church had serious problems just like the church of our day. Take the Corinthians, for example. Many of them were sexually immoral – saved people going to prostitutes. Paul finds this unthinkable, as should you and I. Paul felt that it should not happen even once in all of church history. But, fornication was commonplace then, and it is commonplace now. Some were gluttons and drunks. Lawsuits were frequent between believers who paraded their failures before secular courts rather than resolving their problems privately in the local assembly. Their marriages were failing, they were splitting the one Body into denominations, faking speaking in tongues and abusing other gifts as well, acting selfishly, fighting among themselves, and conducting themselves very much as their unsaved neighbors did. In the Greco-Roman world of the first century, if you wanted to insinuate that someone was a moral reprobate, you called him a "Corinthian," and the early church of Corinth was little different than the surrounding world.

None of these things, however, were the *fundamental* problem in the Corinthian church, they were only symptoms of the problem. The root problem was that their faith was in groupthink, and not in God's Word. Paul wrote to them to correct this major problem we believers have of preferring human "wisdom" to divine wisdom, of following the speculations of men rather than the declarations of God.[1]

When you present the good news of the Grace of Christ[2] to others, they will *OFTEN* object, saying things such as, "But I've always thought..."; "Grandpa used to say..."; "My parents taught me..."; "My pastor believes..."; "My church holds..."; "Dr. So-and-so wrote in his 19 books..."; "The experts feel..."; "The consensus is...", etc. None of this groupthink holds water. God sent angels, prophets, Apostles, pastors and evangelists *ALL* to say, "Thus says the Lord!" not "I prefer to think." Christ on Earth preached the good news of prophecy – "The kingdom of God is at hand,"[3] if you (Israel) will accept it. Israel didn't! He spoke as a Jew under Law to Jews under Law.[4]

Having died for sinners, risen and ascended to the right hand of the Father, the now glorified Christ preached again, this time the good news of the Mystery. What our Lord preached on Earth that we need to know is preserved for us in Matthew, Mark, Luke, and John. What He then spoke from Heaven is recorded in the Epistles of Paul – Romans through Hebrews. His Earthly Kingdom message was the subject of prophecy from time immemorial.[5] His Heavenly Kingdom message was kept secret by God from time immemorial – until He chose to reveal it to and through His chosen vessel, the Apostle Paul.[6] *ALL* of the Bible is *FOR* us – the Pauline Epistles are *TO* us and *ABOUT* us. Check it out! The Mystery communicated to and by our Apostle is the key to understanding the whole Bible from Genesis 1:1 to Revelation 22:21! It is the only truth that can unite the Body of Christ, bringing us all together, and it is the key to living for Christ in a world at war with its own Creator![7]

It is not by accident that Moses towers over all the other Old Testament prophets; he had a unique relationship and ministry to Israel by divine appointment![8] Nor is it accidental that the Dispensation of Grace was committed to Paul singularly, and not to Peter or the Twelve. He is the only one God has told us to follow as he follows Christ.[9]

Do we make too much of Paul? To answer that, we must look at what God makes of him and at what he makes of himself.[10] I Corinthians chapter three would be a good place to start.

"Who, then, is Paul?"[11] is the question the Apostle asks regarding himself as a person, but also concerning his unique Apostleship and distinctive message. Regarding himself personally, he says that he planted (v.6) and that he that plants is *nothing* (v. 7). Zip, zippo, zilch, zero. But God is everything! The Apostle never exalts himself, but *ALWAYS* exalts the Lord! "I am *less than the least* of all saints[12]; I am *the least of the Apostles*;[13] I am *not fit* to be called an Apostle[14]; Christ Jesus came into the world to save sinners, of *whom I am chief [foremost]*[15]...*I am nothing.*"[16]

However, concerning his God-given ministry, he says: "I [singularly] am *the Apostle* to the Gentiles"[17];"The Dispensation of the Grace of God which was *given to me* for you"[18]; "The Dispensation of God which is *given to me* for you, *to complete* the Word of God [with] "the Mystery [secret] which has been hidden from the ages and from the generations, *BUT NOW* was made manifest to His saints."[19]

In his year and a half of ministry to the Corinthians, despite their world-renowned intellectual acumen, the Apostle was unable to take them beyond the baby food of the Word into its adult diet. They preferred pablum to steak – you have to *chew* steak! And the steak of God's Word is the Mystery (secret) divinely disclosed to and through Paul and which can only be communicated by spiritual means.[20] Christian college, university and seminary professors only betray their carnality when they ignore, or even attack, the Mystery with its "deep things of God." Super charged IQs are fine in their place – the natural realm – but absolutely incapable of understanding what can only be taught by and grasped by spiritual means. It is not the Einstein in you that knows God, but the "spiritual man," your new nature![21] "That which has been born of the Spirit is spirit."[22]

The Mystery was not taught by Christ in His earthly ministry because the Twelve were not yet capable of understanding it![23] One commentator wrote, "If there were a secret Rapture, Christ would have told us."[24] Christ *DID* tell us – not in the Gospels, but speaking from Heaven, and our Apostle relays it. "Look, I'm telling you a secret: we shall not all fall asleep, but we shall all be changed, in an instant, in the sparkling of an eye, at the last trumpet; for a trumpet shall sound, and the dead shall be raised incorruptible, and we shall be changed. For this corruption must put on incorruptibility, and this mortal put on immortality. And when this corruption shall have put on incorruptibility, and this mortal shall have put on immortality, then shall come to pass the word that has been written: 'Death was swallowed up in victory.' "[25]

If the people we know are as obstinate in their refusal to accept the special authority of Paul over the Body of Christ as Israel was in rejecting Moses' unique authority over Israel[26], we must lovingly, prayerfully, and carefully invite them to consider these teachings of Scripture:

- The Twelve were saved in Israel, Paul in Gentile Syria.
- Paul, while a Jew, was a Roman citizen.
- Paul did not qualify to be one of the Twelve.[27]
- The Twelve were circumcision Apostles, Paul, an uncircumcision Apostle.[28]
- The Twelve got their Kingdom Gospel from Christ in His humiliation; Paul got his Grace Gospel from Christ in glory.[29]
- The Twelve will govern Israel from Twelve thrones – there is no thirteenth throne![30]
- Paul's Gospel has been preached in "all the world"; the Kingdom Gospel has not.[31]
- The worldwide, Gentile ministry of the Twelve was suspended by God in the Acts period.[32]
- God used only three of the Twelve to write Scripture; they penned only eight Bible books, all intended primarily for Jewish readers.[33]
- God used Paul to write fourteen Bible books – thirteen intended primarily for Gentile readers, one primarily for the Jews.[34]
- Scripture calls Paul uniquely "Apostle to the Gentiles."[35]
- Paul learned the Grace Gospel from Christ risen and glorified; the Twelve learned the Gospel of Grace from Paul.[36]
- The Twelve had known Christ according to the flesh; Paul only knew Christ from Heaven.[37]
- Peter turned his disciples over to Paul.[38]
- In Acts, only one of the Twelve goes to Gentiles, and he (Peter) only to one Gentile, (Cornelius); Paul goes to thousands and thousands of Gentiles.

- ♦ The Twelve were not to "Go...into all the world" until Israel accepts Christ.
- ♦ Paul ALONE introduces and develops "Church truth," the Twelve allude to it after being taught by Paul.
- ♦ The Twelve are sent to baptize, Paul is not.[39]
- ♦ Paul's Apostleship "outranks" that of the Twelve during the present Dispensation of Grace.
- ♦ Paul had more revelations of the risen Christ (personal encounters with Christ) than all Twelve put together.
- ♦ Paul outworked all Twelve. (Not a boast, but a simple statement of fact. Their ministry had been divinely limited to Israel, Paul's had not. This provides us with yet another Dispensational key).
- ♦ Only to Paul is the Dispensation of Grace committed.[40]
- ♦ God tells the Body of Christ to follow Paul, not the Twelve.[41]
- ♦ The Twelve were not able to add to what Paul had learned from Christ; Paul taught the Twelve what they could not learn from Christ.[42]
- ♦ The Twelve "drop through a trap door" one third of the way through the book of Acts; Enter, Paul! They only reappear in connection with and in support of "that new and different Apostle."

There is more, but this ought to keep us busy studying for a while.

When I was an Associate Pastor in a little church in Buffalo Grove, Illinois, the Senior Pastor took seven Sunday evening meetings to teach on "the Seven Dispensations" as found in Scofield's notes. When he got to number six: the Dispensation of Grace, he said "The Twelve seem to drop through a trap door pretty early in Acts; we don't know why." He was a dear man, pastoring a church of dear people, but he *could* have known why. Perhaps he will read this book, and then he *will* know why. Knowing why provides the secret of the Christian life and ministry. I'd say knowing the secret of being faithful in a faithless world is pretty important, wouldn't you?

God kept His secret from eternity past, purposely preventing men and angels from knowing it.[43] Only when the time was ripe for its unveiling did He reveal it to and through His chosen vessel, Paul.[44] The church has never approved of God's choice, and would rather He had spread this authority among the Twelve, much as Israel resented the divine appointment of Moses and even Moses' own brother and sister, in rebellion against God, demanded a piece of the action. But God knew from eternity past that His choice would be Moses for Israel and Paul for the Body of Christ. If we don't like this, tough tomatoes! When the famous evangelist Billy Sunday was told by the village fathers that his preaching was rubbing the fur the wrong way, he answered, "Tell the cat to turn around!"

Error begets error, and truth begets truth. The ancient error that says the Church began on the Day of Pentecost has birthed many offshoot errors that have divided the Church and given us wall-to-wall confusion. With our groupthink mentality, we have tried to continue the program of the Pentecostal church of early Acts which was interrupted when the Jerusalem Jews rejected Christ risen[45], committing the only unpardonable sin, and then "the Jews among the Gentiles" did the same.[46] In Acts, the "sign" nation with its "walk by sight" (lit. "appearance") rejected the ministry of God the Holy Spirit just as their fathers had rejected the ministry of God the Father in the period of the prophets, and the ministry of God the Son in the period of the Gospels. There was no place left for Israel to go, having now rejected Father, Son, and Holy Spirit, and so God turned to the Gentiles, an unprophesied move.[47] According to prophecy, Gentiles were to come to God through Israel's rise, but Israel refused to rise when her time came, so God opened the door of faith to the Gentiles and you and I have come to Him through Israel's fall![48]

And we *are not* the sign nation with its Holy place, priesthood, signs, baptisms, cup of blessing, etc. We walk by faith! We *are not* the church of God of prophecy; we *are* the church of God of Mystery; *we are the Body of Christ!*

Israel's prophetic program will be resumed when our Mystery Program, or Dispensation of Grace, concludes with God's recall of His ambassadors – the translation, or Rapture ("catching away") – of the *PRESENT* church, which has not been "appointed" to wrath (the Tribulation)[49], but has in fact been "delivered from the wrath to come."[50]

Beside the destructive error of starting the "Church which is His Body"[51] as early as Acts two, there is the error of placing the Body under the "sign" nation's "Great Commission." We, the "Body Church" are under a "greater commission" than that given to the Twelve and their followers. OUR commission is to stand in the place of Christ (as His ambassadors) and invite a lost world to "be reconciled to God." God was "in Christ reconciling the world to Himself, not reckoning their offenses to them, and has committed to us the message of reconciliation, now then we are ambassadors for Christ, as it were, God exhorting by us, we entreat for Christ 'be reconciled to God.' "[52]

Does your group teach this "greater commission"? Is your assembly aware of it? Does your pastor realize that all the "new creatures" of verse 17 are under this new and greater commission and cannot be under any of the commissions of Matthew 28, Mark 16, Luke 24, John 20, or Acts 1? If not, don't challenge him, don't undermine his ministry. Give him this book! We cannot be under any commission given to the Twelve for ministry to Israel and the nations any more than they could be under OUR greater commission!

Then there is still another destructive error, perhaps the "mother of all errors" in our time – trying to make Paul one of the Twelve. He never was, nor will he ever be. Paul is "that other and different Apostle" with a unique Apostleship and a distinctive message. He, singularly, is the Apostle for this present economy, or stewardship, of Grace. Some have called it "the Great Parenthesis," some "The Divine Interregnum"; Ephesians calls it "the Dispensation of Grace." It is a program inserted by God Himself into the space which occurs between the temporary suspension of Israel's prophetic program and its resumption, when Israel will fulfill prophecy by becoming the prophesied "kingdom of priests," the "Royal Nation."

Dear Friend, do you see how knowledge of the Mystery (secret) is the key to the Scriptures and the very foundation of all Christian life and ministry? And why God gave "this Grace" to "the less than the least of all the saints" (believers), to "enlighten ALL regarding the fellowship of the secret which has been hidden from the ages in God, who created all things through Jesus Christ, that might be known *NOW*...the multifarious wisdom of God, according to [His] purpose of the ages..."[53]?

Why did God keep His secret a secret until the time was ripe and then unveil it to us – little us? This revelation must be all important to occupy the 14 books of the Bible most relevant to you and me! Have we accepted it? Will we receive it? Or do we, like most believers, love ourselves and our comfort zone more than we love our Lord?

There is no fence here for us to straddle! We must fish or cut bait! Either we permit God to be God and enlighten us through a man who describes himself as a zero and his God as everything, or we refuse to honor God by rendering "the obedience of faith."[54]

Spiritual adultery is, by far, the worst possible kind of adultery, yet if we believe God's prophecy of church history in II Timothy 4:3-4, we must conclude that the church has been committing adultery for 19 centuries, and that you and I are not immune to it. "O Earth, Earth, Earth. Hear the Word of the Lord!"[55]

CHAPTER TWENTY-THREE NOTES

1. I Corinthians 2:5
2. Galatians 1:6
3. Matthew 4:17
4. Romans 15:8
5. Acts 3:18,24
6. Romans 16:25-26; Ephesians 3:1-3,9
7. I Corinthians 1:10
8. Numbers 12:1-9
9. I Corinthians 4:16; 11:1; I Thessalonians 1:6; Philippians 3:17
10. I Corinthians 3:10
11. I Corinthians 3:5
12. Ephesians 3:8
13. I Corinthians 15:9
14. I Corinthians 15:9
15. I Timothy 1:15
16. II Corinthians 12:11
17. Romans 11:13
18. Ephesians 3:2
19. Colossians 1:25
20. I Corinthians ch. 2
21. I Corinthians 2:14-15
22. John 3:6
23. John 16:12-15
24. Oswald Smith
25. I Corinthians 15:51-54
26. Numbers ch. 12
27. Acts 1:21-26
28. Galatians 2:6-9
29. Luke 6:13; 9:1-6; Galatians 1:11
30. Matthew 19:28
31. Romans 1:8; I Thessalonians 1:8; Colossians 1:23; Matthew 24:14
32. Galatians 2:9; Acts 28:25-28
33. Matthew ch. 1; Peter ch. 2; John ch. 5

34. Romans through Hebrews
35. Romans 11:13
36. Galatians 2:6-9 w/ Galatians 1:11012
37. II Corinthians 5:16-17
38. II Peter 3:15-18
39. Matthew 28:19; I Corinthians 1:14-17
40. Ephesians 3:8-9
41. I Corinthians 4:16; 11:1; I Thessalonians 1:6
42. Galatians 2:6-9; II Peter 3:15-18
43. Romans 16:25-61
44. Ephesians 3:9
45. Acts 7:51-54
46. Acts 28:25-28
47. Acts 13:46; 18:6; 28:25-28
48. Isaiah ch. 60 esp. vss 1-3; Romans 11:11-15
49. I Thessalonians 5:9
50. I Thessalonians 1:10
51. Ephesians 1:22-23; Colossians 1:18
52. II Corinthians 5:14-21
53. Ephesians 3:1-11
54. Romans 16:25-26
55. Jeremiah 22:29

CHAPTER TWENTY-FOUR

RIGHTLY DIVIDING THE WORD OF TRUTH

Sometimes, great keys to Bible understanding are missed because the passages that provide them suffer from familiarity. We've heard them so often that we've become innoculated to them and have developed mental antibodies that fight them off. One such passage is II Timothy 2:15 which says, "Be diligent to present yourself to God tested and approved, an unashamed worker, rightly dividing the Word of Truth." This verse appears on the cornerstones and letterheads of churches, colleges, and para-church ministries. We ought to take it very seriously because it is God's injunction to us, and the injunctions of Grace are far more important for us than the injunctions of Law. The Law was temporary, exclusively Israel's, and "not enacted for a righteous person."[1] Grace is our tutor, "... teaching us that, having denied irreverence and worldly cravings, we should constantly live discreetly, and uprightly, and devotedly in this present age...."[2]

If you are saved, you died with Christ, and were raised with Him to resurrection life.[3] Resurrection life can have nothing to do with Law, which was enacted for the unrighteous.[4] The Law is a system of command and penalty, a system of conditional blessing and cursing.[5] The Law was designed for man in the flesh, not for man in the Spirit – not for man in Christ. The great lesson of the Law is that man cannot keep it!

The Law had no claim on Christ. It could not indict Him, arraign Him, or condemn Him. It could not point its bony finger of death at Him – UNTIL HE VOLUNTEERED TO COME UNDER IT to take our sin upon Himself and deliver from Law's curse.[6] Christ lived and died under Law by His own choice, then rose out of it, above it, and beyond it, and He took you with Him.[7]

"But, Jimmy," someone might say, "this chapter was supposed to be about rightly dividing." Yes, but isn't that just what we've been doing? We divided, or *distinguished* between Israel and the Body of Christ, between Law and Grace, between man in the flesh and man in Christ, between Christ in His humiliation and Christ in His glory, and between temporal life and resurrection life. Isn't that a pretty good start?

I once thought that to "rightly divide" meant to recognize that there are 39 books in the Old Testament and 27 in the New, but that isn't true. Most Bible scholars and students agree that Job is the oldest book in the Bible, probably written in Abraham's time, and thus it antedates the old Mosaic covenant – or testament – by four centuries. Genesis concerns man's history before the giving of the Law at Sinai, making it pre-Old Testament Scripture, as are the first 19 chapters of Exodus. So now we have divided the pre-Old Testament Scriptures from the Old Testament Scriptures, but are the Gospels really New Testament? Christ rises out of Law at the *end* of the Gospels; Israel was under Law until August 10th, 70 A.D. when God ceased dealing with Israel as a nation, and the temple came down. Even the Twelve continued to worship in the temple while it stood and to offer animal sacrifices, and circumcise their male children at least thirty years *AFTER* Pentecost![8] The Law was ended *BY* Calvary, but not *AT* Calvary!

To "rightly divide" we must recognize that the four Gospels are Old Testament even though Christ and the Twelve preached the Kingdom Gospel in them, anticipating the New Testament which will be in force in the still-future Earthly Kingdom featured in prophecy. Right division also requires us to recognize that, though we have some blessings in common with the future millennial saints, both covenants – Old and New – God made with Israel and Judah, neither with the Body of Christ![9]

We wrongly divide when, through our ignorance or stubbornness, we fail to grasp the meaning of the Bible's statement to the effect that "We walk by faith, not by sight" (lit. "appearance").[10] Does this imply that Israel was *not* to have faith? No, but it distinguishes God's program for His earthly people from that for His heavenly people. Much of Israel's faith was to come from things seen: the tabernacle with its furnishings – altars, offerings, robed priests, and so on. The Body of Christ is to get its faith from *sola Scriptura* – Scripture alone![11]

Christ rebuked His new "disciples" for trying to make Him king because they "ate of the bread and were filled" and not because they "saw the signs" and were convinced. Israel is the "sign" nation.[12] The prophets predicted that when Messiah came, He would work miracles. Thousands of Jews who believed messianic prophecies, hearing of His signs, wonders, and works of power, turned out to hear Him and were healed. They were *NOT* healed because first century saints had more faith than our generation! A review of the Biblical record will show that *THEY DID NOT*! One famous commentator teaches that were we to have the same amount of faith as the church of early Acts, we would be producing the same mighty miracles. *Baloney! Not so!* Scripture plainly teaches that signs, wonders, and powers belong to Israel's program. Christ never healed so much as a hangnail for His first thirty years on Earth! Not even one common cold! His first miracle was at the wedding in Cana when He was about thirty years of age. All of His mighty signs were performed in the final ten percent of His life! For the first 90%, He must have frequently passed by innumerable blind, lame, deaf, and leprous people. It was simply not His time to produce signs for the "sign people." Our Lord must have had sick, injured, and maimed relatives and friends who went unhealed during this period, some even dying. If Christ healed solely because He is compassionate, we have an impossible enigma. Also, John the Baptist DID NO MIRACLE![13] Did he have no faith, this "greatest born of women"?[14] Signs were a province of an impending kingdom, waiting in the wings. The kingdom won't be "impending" again until the impending Rapture stops pending!

I have a Chinese translation of the Bible. I can't read it. I read English versions. A Bible I don't understand is no better than a Bible I can't read! That's why God tells us to "...study, apply ourselves, be diligent" to rightly divide.[15] We cannot understand God's Word unless we observe the distinctions He has built into it! What *He* distinguishes, *we* must distinguish. "What God has joined, let no one put asunder." Yes, and what God has put asunder, let no one join. If God makes a clear distinction between His program for Israel and His program for the Body of Christ, must we not do so also? Israel's program is the subject of prophecy revealed from the beginning[16]; the Body's program is the subject of the Mystery hidden from the beginning until revealed by Christ through Paul![17]

There are both similarities and differences in their program and provision and ours. If we aren't dividing accurately (lit. "cutting straight"), we are doing so inaccurately to the great ruin of ourselves and others. II Timothy 2:15 says we may be working, but we ought to be blushing. Many Bible teachers have lost the *ability* to feel shame – but not the *necessity*. If you want to be a craftsman without shame, make proper distinctions – "cut straight." God does when He teaches and He wants us to when we teach.

The T.V. peddlers of psychosomatically induced healings for psychosomatically induced illnesses constantly rob Israel of promises made to Israel, and offer them to their audiences indiscriminately. "You will be the head [of the nations] and not the tail"[18] applies to Israel only; the Body of Christ is not, nor will it be a nation. Unsaved Gentiles in "faith healing" audiences can't eat "the children's bread."[19] For 19 years on radio, I offered large sums of money to any faith healer who would meet me at Children's Memorial Hospital and empty the wards. There were no takers.

The most famous male faith healer of the 20th century can't read without his glasses and has lived with painful, crippling arthritis for years. He made daily visits to the hospital in Tulsa to pray for the most famous female healer as she lay dying, but "all the kings horses, and all the king's men" couldn't put her together again! These are two dear people who, I believe, love the Lord. I don't wish to be sarcastic or unkind, but they made shipwreck of the faith of millions of people. So, don't get mad at us'ns, get made at them'uns. Them'uns are indeed dear people and we ought to love them, but God is dearer still, and we ought to love Him *more*. We ought to love Him enough to teach His Word as He meant it to be taught, even if the wishful thinkers are offended. Heresies are destructive to God's people and need to be lovingly opposed.

"What says the Scripture?" was Paul's battle cry! Shouldn't it be ours – yours and mine?

Ouch! Sometimes the Bible hits me like a hammer, and hammers hurt. "Every Scripture is God-breathed and profitable...for correction..." says II Timothy 3:16. I had to learn to enjoy the "hurt" of being corrected. Sometimes God seems to use the most obnoxious Christians to correct us with the Word. It can hurt, but it is necessary. Whenever I have had a tooth pulled, I suffer the pain of dry socket. It can last for hours, or days! But when it's over, I'm always glad that I traded the long term pain of an angry tooth for the short term pain of dentistry.

Don't take doctrinal differences personally. Doing that can cost you opportunities to minister. Beside, it's childish and even stupid. I never get angry unless someone is deliberately attacking my Lord. Even then, I'm careful about how I express my anger. Solomon says it's better to walk away from a fool than to become one yourself! Love people, but love God more.

Was it DeHaan who said, "A Scripture can have but one interpretation, though it may have more than one application"? Peter warned us against interpreting passages that we have isolated from their contexts. "No prophecy of Scripture is of any private [lit. "of its own"] interpretation."[20] Peter believed in dividing correctly. He may have been the chief of "the chiefest Apostles," but he acknowledged that the "new and different Apostle," Paul, had become *his* mentor![21]

A significant key, if I love God and wish to "do His good pleasure," is to observe the distinction God makes in His Word between Israel's Twelve circumcision Apostles and the one uncircumcision Apostle for the Body of Christ. It was quite a shock to me when I learned from Scripture that Israel has Twelve Apostles and I have only one!

Many have learned experientially that even suggesting this can cause a riot in your local church, or in your family, or in your marriage. This Bible truth is part of the Mystery committed *by* God *to* Paul *for* us. The Mystery is all about Grace, and there is nothing that antagonizes the flesh like the Grace of God. In the average church, you can sing, "Grace of God beyond degree" from the choir loft, but don't you dare preach "beyond degree" from the pulpit – or believe it in the pew!

Leonard Heroo said that there are two ways to become unpopular in your local church: one is to sink below the church's level of spirituality, and the other is to rise above it. Rise, brother, rise! Rise, sister, rise! I *do not* mean compete with others to be the most spiritual. That type of competition will only make us the most carnal! Coach John Wooden told his basketball players not to try to be better than others, just to try to be the best that they can be. Paul didn't run to be better than others, but to be the best he could be![22] Is that what *you* are doing? Is it what *I* am doing? It can be!

Paul was willing, like his Lord, to be insulted, brutalized, beaten, tortured, and slain in the service of God. He truly followed in the footsteps of Christ. Millions of believers, including the Twelve, since Paul have done likewise. The 20th century produced more Christian martyrs than the previous 19! No man should stand in a pulpit who is not willing to burn at a stake!

And no man should lead others astray by refusing God's injunction to rightly divide Scripture. The Christian who doesn't rightly divide, wrongly divides, confusing himself, robbing God of His glory, and marginalizing Grace.

Only Grace magnifies God in Christ! May Jesus Christ be praised!

CHAPTER TWENTY-FOUR NOTES

1. I Timothy 1:9
2. Titus 2:11-12
3. Colossians 3:1-3; Romans 6:9-12
4. Romans 7:4
5. Leviticus 26; Deuteronomy 28
6. Galatians 3:13
7. II Corinthians 5:21
8. Acts 21:18-25
9. Jeremiah 31:31-34
10. II Corinthians 5:7
11. Romans 10:17
12. Matthew 16:3; 24:24; Mark 13:22; 16:17,20; Luke 21:11,25; John 4:48; 20:30; Acts 2:19,22,43; 4:30; 5:12; 7:36; 8:13; 14:3; Romans 15:19; II Corinthians 12:12 (2); Hebrews 2:4
13. John 10:41
14. Matthew 11:11
15. II Timothy 2:15
16. Acts 3:8,24,25
17. Ephesians 3:1-5
18. Deuteronomy 28:1,13
19. Matthew 15:21-28
20. II Peter 1:20-21
21. II Peter 3:15-18
22. I Corinthians 9:24-27

Printed in the United States
104124LV00004B/68/A